DUNKELD AND CRAIG-Y-BARNS.

DUNKELD
An Ancient City

LOCAL LORE

PERSONS AND PLACES

By

ELIZABETH STEWART, L.L.A.
DUNKELD

PERTH:
THE MUNRO PRESS, Limited,
36 Tay Street,

"Ye ancient hills, and thou, Duncaledon
Could ye but speak, and tell of friend or foe,
Then would we hear of deeds both strange and great
Deeds that were old, a thousand years ago!"

PREFACE.

My object in placing this book before the public is to give a short and concise history of Dunkeld, along with other points of interest, hoping that this may help to fill a recognised want. So ancient is Dunkeld that its origin is unknown, and its early history borders on the mythical, but I have consulted the best authorities on the subject, and also beg to thank the following gentlemen, who supplied me with scientific and historical notes, viz.:—Messrs. Thos. M'Laren, F.S.A. Scot., Burgh Surveyor, Perth; Davidson Cook, F.S.A. Scot., Barnsley, Yorkshire; H. Mitchell, F.S.A. Scot., Pitlochry; and the Rev. W. M. Tuke, High Wycombe, Bucks.

I gratefully acknowledge the kind permission from the proprietors to reproduce extracts from articles already published by me in the "Weekly Scotsman," the "Glasgow Weekly Herald," the "Dundee Courier and Advertiser," and the "Perthshire Advertiser." Thanks are due for illustrations from Messrs. A. F. MacKenzie, Birnam; H. Coates, F.S.A. Scot., Perth; Davidson, Kirkcaldy; the Dunkeld Mercantile Association; and to the many friends in Dunkeld and elsewhere who assisted me in research and other work.

ELIZABETH STEWART.

Dunkeld, 1926.

CONTENTS.

CONTENTS.

Chapter VIII.

Battle of Dunkeld, 1689; Siege of Blair Castle; Killiecrankie; Cameronians and Highlanders at Dunkeld; Defeat of the latter; Destruction of the Town by Fire; Cathedral Used for Defence and Shelter.

Chapter IX.

Historic Events After 1689; The '15 and the '45; Wade's Roads; Famous Visitors; Visit of Queen Victoria; Free Church; Railway; Prime Minister of Canada's Visit.

Chapter X.

Dunkeld Cathedral; Restoration; Preservation; Existing Monuments.

Chapter XI.

Education—Culdee Settlements; Monastery; Scholarly Abbots and Bishops; School in Chapel of St. George; Foundation of Royal School; Schools and Schoolmasters in 17th Century; Girls' Industrial Schools; Dame Schools.

Chapter XII.

Mackintosh Library; Rev. Donald Mackintosh of Strathtay; His Legacy to Dunkeld; His Life; Last Non-Juring Priest; Inshewan Reading Society.

Chapter XIII.

Dunkeld Bridge; Early Bridges; Present Opened in 1809; Advantages; Toll Riots; View from Bridge.

Chapter XIV.

Decline of Dunkeld; Reformation; Regality and Commissary Courts; Markets; Railway.

Chapter XV.

Parish of Little Dunkeld; Early Bounds; Little Dunkeld Church and Churchyard; Celtic Bell; The Glassites; Gaelic; Ministers.

Chapter XVI.

Birnam; Its Antiquities; Great Birnam Wood; Macbeth; Duncan's Camp; Cup-Marked Rocks; Rohallion Castle; Houghmanstares; Birnam Hill.

Chapter XVII.

Inver; Chapel and Choristers; Niel Gow; Cottage Tree Croft; Dr. Garnett; Collections of Music; Sons; Anecdotes; Tombstone in Little Dunkeld.

Chapter XVIII.

Niel Gow and Burns; Burns' Visit; Controversy on Supposed Epigram; Gow in Dumfries.

ILLUSTRATIONS.

CHAPTER I.

Pre-historic—" Round thee, Duncaledon, the very air feels heavy with
the past, the tale of times that were."—Millar.

DUNKELD had its beginnings ere the written history
of our land began. The misty glamour of an unknown past surrounds its origin. It was the Capital
of the Kaledonoi, a tribe in the midlands of
the ancient kingdom of Pictavia, when the Romans
arrived; but, even at an earlier date, judging from
the stone monuments numerous in the neighbourhood, it was
the tribal resort of an earlier race. Centuries before the advent
of Christianity, and before the Pictish nation emerged from
the darkness of the past, the rude races who wandered o'er
the hills or sheltered in the dense forests found in this
natural stronghold beside the Tay a safe and suitable place
for the performance of religious ceremonials or sepulchral
rites. Records of this are graven on stone, mysterious and
as yet not fully understood, though affording glimpses of
bygone customs, from which modern research is gradually
building up a knowledge of a prehistoric age.

Long before the Picts are surmised to have come from
the Continent to Britain, it is supposed that the land was
inhabited by the Neolithic race, a people of small stature,
copper skins, and dark hair. The stone circles and cup-marked
stones are generally attributed to them, and may either have
been places of worship or of burial. Signs point to both.

Of these, the Dunkeld valley has its share. In the park
near Polney Loch, one mile from Dunkeld, is a Standing
Stone, quite noticeable from the Highland road. This mono-
lith is one of those styled sepulchral, and is a rough oblong
slab of schist, its basal girth being 10 feet 7 inches, and its
height 4 feet 9 inches. Mr. Coles, who describes this
stone in the " Proceedings of the Society of Antiquaries,"
supposes it to have been part of a circle. It is not far from
the ancient stronghold on King's Seat. The same writer also

B

mentions that two other stones of this nature were marked on the Ordnance Survey Map nearer the Cathedral, but he professed himself, after prolonged search, unable to find them. So have others. At Dowally, four miles farther north, are two of a similar kind, massive blocks of quartziferous schist, the highest being 8 feet 9 inches.

Two miles east of Dunkeld are the Standing Stones of Newtyle, commonly called the Druid Stones, near the " Doo's Nest," a projecting crag on the road to Caputh. These Stones were probably monuments before the Druidic period, but the Druids or Pictish Priests generally annexed such monuments, and the name clings through the ages. The Newtyle Stones are possibly remains of a Circle; it is conjectured that, as a spur of Newtyle Hill rises sharply behind, the remainder of the Circle might have been where the road now runs, and had been destroyed during its construction. They are of common quartzose schist differing in height. The largest is over 6 feet at the north corner and 3 feet at the east. A fence divides them from the road; unfortunately, owing to the growth of ferns, bushes, and trees, there is a danger that they may soon be lost to sight. Dr Marshall in his " Historic Scenes of Perthshire " alludes to these two upright stones at the Doo's Nest, but says they are supposed to mark the graves of two Danish warriors returning from the invasion of Dunkeld. Antiquarian research, however, as reported in the Society's Proceedings, places them among pre-historic monuments.

At Easter Cults, a mile or two beyond Newtyle, is a re-markable group of stones, consisting of two upright and one prostrate, placed on a ridge running east and west, at a height of 668 feet above sea-level, commanding a magnificent view of the wide Howe of Strathmore. The larger standing stone is 9 feet high, broad at the base, the other not much smaller. The third is cup-marked, over 2 feet in height, sloping towards the ground, its broad surface pitted all over with groups of cups, those strange indentations with con-centric circles and connecting lines which have puzzled many wise and learned men. The groupings, some hold, are astronomical; others contend that they record great events of the past, whilst one fanciful theory has it that the cups are hollows in which water libations were poured to the Sun-God. On this stone there are about 158 cup-shaped depressions, varying in diameter from 1 to 4 inches. There seems no special design in the arrangement of the cups, and none are surrounded by rings, a common feature in some cases. The three stones are rough unhewn blocks of metamorphic slate of greenish hue, but the colouring is varied on the prostrate one, probably owing in part to weather protection. One writer suggests that there are indications of these three forming part of a huge circle about 78 feet in diameter, an uncommon size in Perthshire.

Near the Slate Quarries on Birnam Hill are two other groups of cupmarks. On the upper surface of one rock is a group of twenty well formed and deeply cut. On a detached mass near is a second group. These sculpturings are more fully described in Chapter 16, " Birnam." Another cup-marked stone is at Kincairney, near the site of an ancient chapel, the foundations of which are almost covered with turf. Still another is at Cardney, and, in addition, are numerous cairns, standing stones, and remains of circles on Ben-e-challie and in Strathbraan. Some would even include the famous Rocking Stone on the top of Craig-y-barns in the collection of ancient monuments, occupying, as it does, such a prominent site. Geologists, however, claim it as a perched boulder, relic of the Ice Age, but this does not altogether preclude the possibility that it might have been in use as a rude altar for the worship of the sun. Near Meikle Obney, beyond Birnam, is a Standing Stone to which a curious legend is attached. A witch flying through the air on a Satanic behest had this stone in her lap, and it fell, hence it is termed the Witch's Stone.

Whilst these various stone monuments confirm the idea that Dunkeld had the makings of a community in very early ages, the name itself suggests considerable antiquity, and has been the subject of much conjecture and dispute. In the Statistical Accounts of Scotland, dated 1798, the name is mentioned as Dunkeldin, Dunchald, or Dunchalden, derived from Dunghaeldhun, meaning the Stronghold of the Gaels or the Hazels. Dr Marshall in " Historic Scenes " also derives the name from the Gaelic Dunghaildhun, thence to Duncalidon, interpreting this as the fort of the Gaels, which he states was probably situated on the King's Seat. This is a small terraced hill, a spur of Craig-y-barns, bearing the remains of an old fort, said to be the abode of Pictish Royalty from 446 to 843 A.D. But Buchanan, the Scottish historian, makes out that Dunchalden, or Hill of the Hazels,

is the mound known as Stanley Hill, near the Cathedral.
Anciently this was, he says, a small knoll where the town's
children amused themselves by wrestling and other games,
it being then named the Shawkie Hill, or, as it is referred to
in certain old registers, the " Shiochie's Hill, a little hillock
within the City of Dunkeld." To understand this assertion
it must be remembered that the position of Dunkeld has
changed more than once. Before the battle of 1689 the
town stretched westwards at least five acres beyond the
Cathedral. In 1690, it was rebuilt towards the east, and
former parts of the town, such as the hillock in question, are
now within the ducal policies. This mound was afterwards
heightened and terraced in military fashion, in imitation of
German fortifications, by the Dukes of Atholl, and cannon
placed on the ramparts.

A third derivation is supplied by David Millar, author of
a poem entitled " The Tay," published at Perth in 1850.
According to him, Duncaledon or Dunkelden, the ancient
form of the present name, signifies the stronghold of the
rough, mountainous country.

MacLean's Guide, " Dunkeld; Its Straths and Glens,"
derives the name from the ancient British words " Dun-
kaled-in or Caledonia or Dunchuildich, signifying the "Stronghold of the Culdees." This latter is an unlikely derivation,
as there was a fort prior to the establishment of the Culdee
faith. The same objection applies to another derivation
sometimes offered, viz., " Dunchailin," from Dun, a hill, and
" cailin," a maid, whence " Hill of the Virgin Mary." A
last version is Dunchallion, " City of the Forests."

Dunkeld, because of its situation on the verge of a great
mountain barrier, with an opening towards verdant plains,
naturally enough became a place of strategic importance.
The appellation, " Gates of the Mountains," was applied
to the Pass formed by Birnam and Newtyle Hills on either
side of the Tay. These hills, with Craig-y-barns and Craigvinean, enclose Dunkeld, forming a natural stronghold, and
it is not therefore surprising to find that the warlike Picts
established a fort or castle there. This Castle of Caledon
was probably one of the first civic centres in Scotland. It
was the capital of a Pictish State, and a residence of Pictish
kings. The King's Seat is generally supposed to have been
the stronghold, the remains of fortifications and outworks
strengthening this belief, and tradition also avers that a

skirmish of some kind took place near it. To the south is the
" Pley Burn," interpreted locally as " The burn of discord or
quarrel." The castle or residence was important enough to
bring the Romans to the vicinity, though they did not
penetrate far enough to attempt its capture. The Roman
Camp at Inchtuthill, six miles from Dunkeld, was constructed
by Agricola in 84 A.D. Recent excavations show that the
Romans remained a considerable time in this camp, and it is
considered highly probable that their objective was the Pictish
stronghold at Dunkeld. Inchtuthill was one of the Roman
posts or stations which commanded the whole of the Stormont
and every road which could lead the Caledonians or northern
tribes down from Atholl and Glenshee into the countries
below.

Distinct from this Roman Camp at Inchtuthill is a British
fort at the west end of the island, older than the Roman
occupation.

The Dunkeld stronghold or castle of Caledon was menaced
several times by the Romans, but unsuccessfully. One of the
early dates of an unsuccessful invasion is 138 A.D.

Scanty and meagre is the knowledge of these early Picts,
who appear to have been simply a number of warlike tribes
with various strongholds or capitals, of which Dunkeld
formed one. The town, if such it could be named, would
possibly resemble other Pictish settlements, and be a circle of
low, rude, roofless huts. The Castle, though claiming to be
an abode of royalty, would be little better, but would possess
fortifications, probably of stone, or, it may be, partly earthen.

CHAPTER II.

Early Christian: Culdees.

THE sun-worship of the early tribes of Scotland was superseded by Christianity in the 5th and 6th centuries. Probably the Roman invaders brought the glad tidings even earlier, but only in isolated cases was it found. As the Northern Celts or Picts had already appropriated the altars and monuments of their predecessors, so they appropriated the festivals and saints of the new religion. The Pictish priesthood or Druids do not appear to have been very ardent objectors to the new faith, and simply retained their pagan customs and deities by giving them new names. Examples of this are found all over the country, and one good example is found in the history of the well-known wishing or healing well five miles from Dunkeld. It is commonly called the Grews Well, a supposed corruption of Sancta Crux or Well of the Holy Cross. Its efficacy was greatest on the first Sunday of May (Old Style), and the date suggests, when considered along with the pilgrimage to it and the rites practised then, that it is obviously a survival of a Pagan or Beltane feast to welcome the advent of summer. Another example is that of the Standing Stone at Staredam, three miles from Birnam. On it is an incised cross, and the Society of Antiquaries report that this is one of the first instances on record in which the symbol of the Christian faith is placed on a stone clearly a member of a pre-historic group.

Early Christian missionaries to the Valley of the Tay were St. Ninian and St. Colm, the latter often confused with St. Columba. St. Ninian was the son of a Pictish Galloway chief, and was sent to Rome as a boy. His missionary travels took place early in the 5th century. A chapel was dedicated to him centuries after in Dunkeld, and a small by-way running off Atholl Street still bears the name St. Ninian's Lane, but there is no record that he visited Dunkeld. The greatest early Christian missionary was St. Columba, to whom the Dunkeld Cathedral is dedicated, and who became the Patron Saint of Dunkeld.

The foundation of Dunkeld as a recognised ecclesiastical centre dates from a later period than its civic; the latter was probably the cause of the first. Vague and contradictory are the accounts of its early religious settlements, and some of these accounts, long accepted, are now regarded as inaccurate.

In various guides and early accounts of Dunkeld, a Culdee settlement is said to have been founded in 570 A.D. by Conal, the 5th King of the Dalreadic Scots in Argyle, a kinsman of St. Columba, but some attribute it to Bridei, a king of the Picts and a convert of the Saint. Neither of these statements are accepted by later authorities. The historian Holinshed, writing in the 16th century, says that "Kentigern (St. Mungo) went with St. Colme unto the Castell of Calidon (otherwise called Dunkeld), where they remained six months in a Monastery there builded by King Convall, teaching and preaching unto the people of Atholl, Caledon and Angus, that in great numbers came unto them to hear their godlie instruction."

St. Colme is used here for St. Columba. Holinshed's account is not accepted as accurate in these particulars. Columba and St. Mungo may have met in the valley of the Tay, each bent on missionary enterprise, but they did not travel together. The following particulars as to the establishment of a religious settlement in Dunkeld have been carefully culled from authoritative works such as Skene's Celtic Scotland, Hume Brown's History, and later works on the Pictish People founded on the oldest Chronicles extant. The earliest writing bearing reference to Dunkeld is the Scalacronica which quotes the Pictish Chronicle and the Chronicles of Loch Leven.

St. Columba, the Apostle to the Highlands, was born in Co. Donegal, Ireland, on the 7th December, 521 A.D. He came to Iona in 560 with twelve companions, eager to convert the various Pictish tribes to Christianity. He travelled throughout Scotland and went on a mission to the Pictish Court, near Inverness, establishing monasteries in many districts, all subject to Iona. In early written manuscripts of his life, descriptions of these journeys are given, and there is no mention of a visit to Dunkeld, but it is related that he went a " circuit of instruction among the men of Alba " and that he taught the tribes about the mouth of the Tay. He was mentioned, on his death, as the teacher of the " tribes of Toi, a river in Alban." He died in 597. About 600 the Dalriadic Scots founded a Collegiate Church which, in the MS. of St. Adamnan (contained in the British Museum), is called the " Muintir Kailli-an-Find," after St. Fintan, a youthful disciple of St. Columba. The exact site is unknown, but it was in the valley of the upper Tay, near but above Dunkeld. " Muintir " was the name given to these families of monks, which consisted of twelve members on the model of the Apostolic band. These " muintirs " became later, college centres of education. St. Fintan is said to have fallen ill at the one above Dunkeld, and remained there for a time. In describing this Collegiate Settlement near Dunkeld as the Muintir Kailli-an-Find, the supposition is that the scribe is intending to translate the Latin into the Celtic tongue and that the name means the "Muintir of St. Fintan" among the Callen (Chaillin) or Caledonians, whose capital was Dun-callen, now Dunkeld.

A Bishop missionary among the Britons, Saxons, and Picts was St. Marnoc, who died in 625. He also founded churches. The name Dalmarnock in Little Dunkeld Parish perpetuates his memory there.

It may therefore be conceded that if St. Columba himself did not reside and preach in Dunkeld, one of his disciples settled near, and so from that period the religious foundation of Dunkeld may be said to have begun. St. Columba, from his gentle demeanour, was surnamed the " Dove," and Dunkeld in choosing him for its patron Saint recognises the name in its armorial bearings:—" Sable, a dove argent, holding in its beak an olive branch, the shield surrounded by a ribbon, whereon is written Caledonia; at the bottom, a thistle, the whole encircled by two palm branches, vert."

The Saint was a diligent transcriber, being credited with the writing of three hundred books. Two specimens are still extant, the Book of Darrow and the Psalter known as the " Battler," because it was borne to battle as a victory-winning relic. This latter is written in small, round hand, with the initial letters larger than the text, and is preserved in a Cathac or Silver Shrine of 11th century work, in the Museum of the Royal Academy, Dublin.

Canon Myln, in The Lives of the Bishops of Dunkeld, written early in the 16th century, does not allude to this religious establishment of St. Fintan. Writing of the origin of the See of Dunkeld, he says, " from his affection to St. Colme, the guardian of Scotland, Constantine III., by the persuasion of St. Adampanus, built and endowed a Convent upon the banks of the Tay, about the year 729. . . . . In this convent he placed that sort of monks, which are commonly called Kelidees or Colidees, that is, worshippers of God."

Adampanus is probably intended for Adamnan.

It is noticeable that the name ' Culdees ' is not applied to the Columban monks until the 8th century. Indeed, the name is said to have originated with Hector Boece, an early historian whose history is mainly fabulous. A distinction is even sometimes drawn between Columba's followers and the Culdees, the latter superseding the former, even as Columba's Irish-Scot ecclesiastical foundations had supplanted those of St. Ninian, the Pictish missionary. This is a perplexing and obscure period. The inhabitants of North Britain were termed Caledonians or Picts indifferently. The very names of the kings are given variously, and dates are uncertain.

Constantin I., the son of Urguis, reigned from 789 till 820. Neither he nor any successor could therefore have established a Convent or Monastery at Dunkeld in 729, yet there seems to have been one of a kind, about and before that period, of which St. Adamnan, the 9th Abbot of Iona, is sometimes said to have been the first Abbot. This Saint died in 704, so could not have used persuasion in 729. He compiled a biography of Columba, founded on an earlier work, which contains in the midst of much that is incredible, valuable information concerning ancient ecclesiastical affairs.

In this biography, Columba is extolled as more than man. Gates flew open at his approach; the sick were restored to health. " Angelic in appearance, Columba was graceful in speech, holy in work, with talents of the highest order. He never could spend even the space of one hour without study or prayer or writing or some other holy occupation."

St. Adamnan describes how the first settlements were made in Iona, and how the monks went for boatloads of branches which they interlaced and made into wattles for the construction of a church or school. The same primitive arrangements would naturally prevail in the early Dunkeld settlement, which was probably a continuation of the " Fintan Muintir " in the neighbourhood. These settlements were entirely different from those of Rome, and the monks were really hermits, or a kind of secular clergy, not necessarily celibate. Adamnan describes the simple dress of the monks, and how they wore shoes of hide, and had separate cells or " bee-hive " dwellings, the whole being surrounded by a " rath " or " cashel," that is, a circular wall of earth or stone. The buildings were all constructed of wattles, twigs plastered with mud.

One can picture Dunkeld in these days. There would be the same pleasant valley and thick woods, and the same majestic river, but all else was different. Wild beasts, now extinct in Scotland, roamed the forests, and were hunted eagerly; the Picts could weave, but the skins of animals were the general coverings of the people. In and near the " Castle of Caledon " would stride painted warriors, fierce, and tattooed strangely; mixing with them, as the Druidic priesthood vanished, were those early Christian teachers, teaching and preaching, yet occupied in manual labour, for they built their own dwellings and found their own food. Iona had corn fields and orchards. It is not to be supposed that the Dunkeld settlement would be neglected in this respect, and, indeed, tradition connects monks with the steep braes behind Dunkeld, named of old, the sunny braes.

The first actual church foundation in Dunkeld was in the time of Constantin I., King of the Picts, who built a church of stone there. It may be about the year 810, but again dates conflict.

Wyntoun, Prior of Lochleven in the 14th century, thus writes in his " Orygynale Cronykil ":—

> " The Kyng off Peychtis, Constantyn,
> Be Tay than founded Dwnkelydyne,
> A place solempne Cathedrale in
> Awcht hundyr wyntyr and fyftene."

The Kingdom of Pictavia was beginning to totter in these days, and the Picts were retreating before the Scots, a tribe who had come from Ireland. They had also trouble with other invaders. In 834, the Picts mustered a large army and occupied the Castle of Caledon, but in 839, owing to the complete destruction of their Royal House in a battle with the Vikings, Kenneth MacAlpine of Galloway became King of the Scots and Picts combined. In 848 or 850, he enlarged and re-built Constantin's Church at Dunkeld, selecting it as central for the whole kingdom. To it also he removed from Iona the relics of St. Columba, deeming the inland church safer from the ravages of the Danes than Iona. He constituted Dunkeld an Annoid or Mother Church, over the Columbans in Scotland, and resolved to place the Abbot of the New Monastery of Dunkeld as Bishop over the Church in the southern territories, with a view to one bishop all over the kingdom. Fortrenn was the name of the kingdom of the Southern Picts. The Abbot of Dunkeld, receiving the title of the Bishop of Fortrenn was thereby recognised as the Head of the Pictish Church; as the Abbot of Dunkeld, he was the guardian of St. Columba's relics, and so was, by common consent, regarded as head of the Columban Church. In this manner, therefore, Dunkeld held the Primacy and became head of the Christian Church in Scotland for a short period. Abernethy next held the Primacy, which was afterwards removed to St. Andrews. Thus Kenneth MacAlpine's scheme of the Dunkeld Episcopal Primacy failed, chiefly owing to the displeasure of the Scottish clergy, who were rapidly becoming Romanised and did not wish the supremacy of the Columban faith which was recognised and followed at Dunkeld.

The Dunkeld Monastery had many famous Abbots. There was Adamnan, biographer of St. Columba. His name was remembered in Dunkeld, for " Dunkeld House " or the " Cottage," demolished in 1900, which stood near the Cathedral, originally bore the appellation of St. Adamnan's Cottage. Then there was St. Moroc to whom a chapel was dedicated near Ballinluig. Ethelred, brother of King Edgar, was another Dunkeld Abbot, and in the Annals of Ulster are notices of several. Tuathal MacArtgu is mentioned as Chief Bishop of Fortrenn and Abbot of Duncaillon, 850-864 A.D. Duncha, still another, was slain at the Battle of Duncrub in Strathearn, in an attempt to dethrone Duff, son of Malcolm II., but the Abbot who has left the chief abiding mark on history, because of his descendants, was Crinan.

Crinan, Lay Abbot of Dunkeld, and son of the Lord of the Isles, married Bethoc, daughter of Malcolm II. Their son was the unhappy Duncan, who figures in Shakespeare's tragedy of " Macbeth," and whose son afterwards became Malcolm III., or Malcolm Canmohr. Crinan is therefore one of the ancestors of our Royal family. It is remarkable, too, that through his descendants, the religious order of Scotland was changed. Canmohr married the Saxon Princess Margaret, whose influence on the side of the Church of Rome helped to suppress the simpler Culdee faith.

Dunkeld, although inland, was not long exempt from the Danes, who troubled the whole island. In 845, Kenneth MacAlpine defeated them near Clunie Loch, as they were marching on to plunder Dunkeld. In spite of this defeat, repeated attacks were made on the city. In the reign of Constantin III., who succeeded in 904, Dunkeld was plundered. One Danish leader, Regner Lodbrog, King of Denmark, afterwards met with a terrible death, being thrown into a dungeon filled with vipers by order of the King of Northumbria, but so dauntless was he that he composed and sang his celebrated death-song in which he refers to the sacking of Dunkeld. The Danes were finally defeated at Luncarty by Kenneth III., who came to the throne in 970 A.D.

The total destruction of " Duncaillen in Alba " in 1027 is recorded in the Annals of Ulster.

There are several relics of this early Christian period in Dunkeld and neighbourhood. One of four Celtic bronze bells found in Scotland, is preserved in Little Dunkeld Church. It is more fully described in the chapter on " Little Dunkeld."

In " Early Christian Monuments," published in 1903, by J. Romilly Allen, C.E., F.S.A. (Scot.), there are descriptions of various stones in Dunkeld belonging to this period, and also in Stuart's " Sculptured Stones of Scotland."

No. 1 is in the Ducal policies, near Dunkeld House, not far from St. Colme's Well and the King's Seat. It is a slab of grey sandstone, 3 ft. 6 in. by 1 ft. 9 in., lying flat on the ground. The sculpturing consists of the incised figure of a man on horseback, blowing a horn, with spear in the right hand. A Dunkeld writer, writing in 1842, says that this stone turned up a few years before then in a field, the figure carved on it being hailed then as that of a Roman warrior. If it had lain for ages there, it may indicate the unknown site of Fintan's Muintir, or Collegiate Settlement.

In Dunkeld Cathedral there are two stones, both badly placed for observation behind the screen.

One is a slab of red sandstone, with an incised inverted Cross on one side, the other is of grey sandstone, sculptured in relief on four faces. Both were used for a time as gate-posts at the entrance to the side of the Cathedral, and marks of this usage still remain.

The grey sandstone is nearly rectangular in shape, 4 ft. 10 in. by 2 ft. 6 in. by 1 ft. 1½ in. thick. Mr Romilly Allen describes it thus:—Front (Apparently this is now turned to the back and cannot be seen).—The remains of what appears to have been a Cross on one panel containing a figure subject consisting of 2 horsemen riding, a row of 4 men, 3 more prostrate on the ground, one decapitated—a man between 4 beasts, probably intended for Daniel in the Den of Lions . . .

Back (now the front).—Divided in 3 panels. At the top is a figure subject consisting of 16 or more heads representing a crowd and a circular disc. This might be the Miracle of the Loaves and the Fishes, disc representing loaves. Below, the 12 Apostles. Right side (left).—One panel only remaining at top, man on horseback; below, 3 men. Left side (right).—Defaced; a scroll of foliage.

Dr. Joseph Anderson suggests that the crowd on stone resembles a confused group of chariots and horsemen, so might be the engulfing of Pharaoh's host in the Red Sea with Israelites on shore and representatives of the 12 tribes of Israel. He says the sculpture, though more rudely executed, resembles this subject engraved on a fragment of the sarcophagus at Arles. Another authority has it that the disc is neither loaves nor chariot wheels, but the stone rolled away from the Sepulchre.

There are two beautiful engravings of this stone in the Papers of the Spalding Club, to be seen in the Reference Library of the Albert Institute, Dundee.

These sculpturings probably belong to the 8th or 9th Centuries and are examples of Pictish art. Those " People of the Woods " were an emotional and imaginative race, as well as warlike, worshipping Nature and loving to depict natural objects, using such as symbols and signs, and mingling birds and beasts with the sign of the Christian faith, when they accepted the new religion.

CHAPTER III.

DUNKELD CATHEDRAL.

Foundations and Early History.

THE relics of St. Columba thus deposited in the church founded by Constantin I., and rebuilt by Kenneth MacAlpine, gave Dunkeld a peculiar and honourable position, even after the primacy was transferred to Abernethy. These relics afterwards became suspiciously abundant and were found in various parts of the country. Skene, the historian, says some were sent to Ireland for safety in 878, but were restored to Iona in 900 A.D. However, Dunkeld retained its share until the Reformation. In the 11th century the Celtic Abbacy of Dunkeld had become an appanage of the Crown and subsequently descended to the Earls of Fife. In 1127, the Culdee Monastery or Church at Dunkeld was changed into a Cathedral Church by "St. David" or King David I., son of Malcolm III. and Margaret. The Book of Deer, preserved in Cambridge, shows the original charter granted by David to the Cathedral, and is a translation from the Latin into Gaelic, the language then of Scotland. The Culdee Corporation was constituted a body of secular clergy when Gregory, their Abbot, was made first Bishop of the remodelled See of Dunkeld, and the new Cathedral supplied with Augustinian Canons appointed by Rome. This Culdee Corporation existed side by side with the Canons Regular of St. Augustine for two centuries.

The nature or form of this first Cathedral Church is unknown, but part of the present edifice is reared on the site of the old. The stones were retained and are yet easily discernible in the eastern gable, forming an irregular reddish streak in the midst of preponderating grey.

Occupying a position of strategic importance combined with much natural beauty and ruled by a number of illustrious and distinguished prelates, members of influential Scottish families, Dunkeld Cathedral long held a prominent place in the annals of Scottish ecclesiastical history.

It stood on the borders of almost unknown ground to the Southern Scot, and was exposed to fierce assaults by men who cared for none of these things. In their pathless mountain fastnesses what recked the clansmen and their chiefs of monk, priest or bishop? They came down in their fury when they listed and even robbed the pilgrim to the sacred shrine of his offering. The marvel is that any part of the building is still standing to commemorate the piety of those who reared it. With little pretensions to size or architecture when compared with structures elsewhere, it yet remains a wonderful monument to the skill, patience and courage of the men of old. They chose a romantic, beautiful spot on the banks of a mighty river, and it is but fitting that reverence should be paid to their memory. The oldest part of the present building is the Choir, founded in 1318 by Bishop Sinclair. The revenues are said to have been considerable at that period. Holinshed has it, " There is a church in the same place where the said Castell of Calidon sometime stood, a church dedicated unto St. Colme, built of faire, square stones, being at this day a Bishop's See, commonlie called Dunkeld, indowed with manie faire revenues and great possessions for the maintenance of the bishop and his cannons."

The Bishops of Dunkeld were important personages in Scotland. In the Chapter House of Westminster there are seven of the Seals of Bishops of Dunkeld appended to documents preserved there. The oldest is attached to a parchment dated the 25 May, 1303. A description of another Seal is given by Henry Laing in his valuable work of seals, " The Seal of Causes of the Chapter of Dunkeld. A Round Seal of excellent work. . . . A figure of St. Columba, with nimbus, in pontifical vestments, sitting on a plain throne. . . . At

each side . . . is a half-length figure of an angel waving
the thurible and the words S. Columba."

The Bishops had palaces or residences in Edinburgh,
Perth, Clunie and Dunkeld. Clunie Castle still remains, but
that in Dunkeld has vanished. In St. John's Street, Perth,
there was placed in 1926, a beautifully executed panel on the
first floor of the business premises occupied by Messrs. Laing
& Co. The inscription records that " The House of the
Bishops of Dunkeld stood behind these buildings in a garden.
. . . This house was erected prior to 1461, and was demolished
in 1821 A.D.

Gavin Douglas, Bishop of Dunkeld (B. 1474, D. 1522)
          In a barbarous age,
Gave to rude Scotland, Virgil's page."

The Diocese included large sections of Perthshire and
Forfarshire; such as the Cally District, near Blairgowrie, the
burying ground at the Steps of Cally being attached to one
of their chapels. In the Lothians, Preston, Bonkill, Aberlady,
Abercorn, Cramond and Inchcolm were dominical lands of
Dunkeld.

After the Choir, founded in 1318, the Nave followed. This
was begun in 1406 by Bishop Cardney and finished in 1448 by
Bishop Ralston, who began the Aisles. This latter bishop was
so zealous in the cause that he himself carried, and made his
visitors do likewise, stones from Gellyburn Quarry, six miles
distant. These stones are all of small size, and the transport
was very difficult, there being no proper road to the quarry,
so that most of the stones were carried in creels on horseback.

The building thus founded and completed by various
bishops at various dates gives evidence of this by its mixed
architecture, Gothic and Norman. It consists of an aisleless
Choir, a Nave with two aisles, towers and Chapterhouse.
The latter has been converted into a Mausoleum for the
Atholl family, and contains several Renaissance Monuments.
It was founded or heightened by Bishop Lauder, and bears
his arms, griffin, sergeant, carved. There is a wheel stair,
a recessed tomb, carved stones and an 18th century Monument with 32 Coats of Arms.

DUNKELD CATHEDRAL.
[Photo by A. F. Mackenzie, Birnam.

ST. ADAMNAN'S COTTAGE—Taken down in 1878.
[Photo by A. F. Mackenzie, Birnam.

The high Gothic open arch between Nave and Choir is built up. The main aisle is separated from the side ones by six round pillars of Norman design, the intervals terminating in sharp arches of the Second Style of Gothic. The windows lighting the aisles are all different, showing great diversity of design. The West Window has been formed in a very elaborate pattern, but a curious feature is its want of symmetry, the little florid cross which terminates the gable being away from the centre, showing an unusual and lop-sided appearance. The small rose window near is beautiful in design, and so also is the tower on the Southern Angle with its rose-carved mouldings and parapet, perforated by panelled quartrefoils.

The North-West Tower is 96 feet high, and is good and simple in design. The ground floor is vaulted and has been painted. In the outer wall was a curious zig-zag rent from top to bottom, alluded to by Pennant in his " Travels," 1772. It is now filled up. The Tower is entered from the Nave. Passing through a small door near the West Window, the ascent is made by a winding spiral stairway, lately put in thorough repair. The view from the top is of surpassing beauty. The spectator looks down upon a beautiful vale, through which rolls the River Tay, bordered by gardens, shrubberies, and verdant meads, and spanned by its picturesque Bridge. The great swelling parks are studded with magnificent trees, while Dunkeld and Birnam lie open to the gaze, at the base of sheltering guardian hills.

The basement of the Tower was formerly used for the Commissary Court, and in the top is a Chime of Bells placed by the Atholl family. Bishop Brown is recorded to have placed four or five bells in the Steeple. On one was an inscription, but the bell was broken and cast anew in 1688, another inscription replacing it, mentioning Bishop Brown. The greater bell was named St. Colme. A window in the North-West corner of the Nave has this Bishop's Coat of Arms—a chevron between three fleurs-de-lys—and is surmounted by a mitre. The inscriptions on a ribbon round the Arms is very minute.

c

A very full description with architectural details of this noble building is to be found in " Ecclesiastical Architecture " by Mac Gibbon and Ross; also in MacLean's Guide to Dunkeld. Masonic Marks are said to have been found by the brethren on various parts.

Near the Cathedral to the South-West stood the Bishop's Palace, which does not appear to have been of any special workmanship. It is said to have consisted of several long houses, two stories high with thatched roof, but a strong Castle was built near it by Bishop Cardney as a place of defence. In it was a great hall with vaulted granaries and larders beneath. This Castle has completely disappeared, but the site was long known as Castle Close. Men drilled there as late as the year 1716.

Subterranean passages, connecting Palace and Cathedral and residences of other clergy, existed, and traces of such were found not so very long ago.

The Anglicising process of the Scottish Church began in the 11th Century, when the Culdee gave way altogether to Rome, and the Orders of the Cathedral were copied from types in England. The Chapter of Dunkeld took Salisbury as guide, and consisted of Bishop, Deans, Prebendaries and other officials. At the request of Bishop Lauder (1452-75) James II. erected the lands of the Bishopric north of the Forth into a barony called the barony of Dunkeld (Dowden's Bishops of Scotland) and in 1577, after the Reformation, James, Bishop of Dunkeld, appointed the Earl of Atholl and his heirs to the office of " heretable Baillerie " of the lands of the Barony of Dunkeld charging the salary of the post on the lands of " Eister and Wester Insheweyns and Ladiewell." This was done by the consent of Dean and Chapter.

The Columban relics, including the bones of the Saint, his books, staff and stone pillow, were kept in safe custody in the Cathedral, objects of much reverence, but at the Reformation they were carried off, some suppose by the Roman clergy, to Ireland, where, indeed, at this day, Columba's bones are said to be.

This Anglicising or Romanising of the Culdee Church is offered as one of the reasons why the Celtic Bell in Little

Dunkeld Church is not preserved in the Cathedral, which occupies the site of the original Culdee settlement. Little Dunkeld Church was the parish church of the district, Minor or Lesser Dunkeld; the City of Dunkeld with the Cathedral being Major or Meikle. The Parish Church, retaining the older associations, possibly thus retained the bell, for the Augustinian Canons regarded Culdeeism as heresy, refusing to venerate the relics or saints of that faith.

CHAPTER IV.

Myln's " Lives of the Bishops of Dunkeld.

A VERY valuable and realistic description of the Lives and Works of the Bishops of Dunkeld is contained in the MS. written and compiled by Alexander Myln, a Canon and Official of Dunkeld and Prebendary of Moneydie at the time of writing. He afterwards became Abbot of Cambuskenneth and first President of the College of Justice. The manuscript is styled " Vitæ Dunkeldensis Ecclesiæ Episcoporum a prima sedis Fundatione ad. an. 1515 ab Alex. Myln," A copy from the original has been printed in Latin. A translation has also been printed from a copy written about the beginning of the 18th Century by a writer who, from internal evidence, appears to have been well acquainted with the places mentioned. This translation is printed with other ancient records in the 1st Volume of the Transactions of the Literary and Antiquarian Society, Perth, published in 1827. Copies can be seen in the Reading Rooms of Dunkeld and Birnam.

The work is of considerable value, as it gives a history of the See of Dunkeld, as he understood it, from 729 A.D. to 1515, and describes the process of the erection of Dunkeld Cathedral, with dates, also enumerating in great detail the various ornaments and valuables, once cherished possessions. Very quaint and amusing, too, are his word pictures of the Bishops and others of the clergy. With a few graphic touches he depicts the man.

In the beginning, Canon Myln explains his reason for writing. He tells that, having observed the magnificent ornaments of the Cathedral and of the churchmen, he desired to know who were " the authors of that fine system which gave rise to that spirit of devotion and good government which reigns here." He therefore searched the old writings of the church, the records of the kingdom and the registers of the Abbeys, so as to be " distinctly informed of the names of our prelates and other great men who gave rise to that spacious and elegant church."

Opening by giving a list of all the church officials at the time, he describes the foundation of the Culdee Monastery, attributing it to Constantin III., " by the persuasion of St. Adampanus," but there is evidently some confusion over names and dates here, as shown in the previous chapter. " This Convent, my reverend fathers," says Myln, " stood partly where at present your eastern garden is, and partly where the Manse of Crief now stands. . . . Upon the increase of devotion among princes, the good King David . . . changed this into a convent of seculars at the same time he got appointed a bishop and canons about the year 1127."

Thus Myln briefly alludes to the suppression of the Culdees—an Order of which Renan, the great French scholar, says, " Few forms of Christianity have offered an ideal of Christian perfection so pure as the Celtic Church of the sixth, seventh and eighth centuries. Nowhere, perhaps, has God been better worshipped in spirit than in the great communities of Iona, Bangor and others."

The MS. contains a long list of Bishops, concluding with the ordination of Gavin Douglas. The account of the work, the benefactions and trials of these men is a striking picture of clerical life in early times.

The following extracts speak for themselves :—" Bishop Galfred had a great zeal for the worship of God. . . . There were few of the canons who before this time resided at Dunkeld, and the musick of the quire was not agreeable to the Gregorian manner. Therefore to make the canons attend better he qualified his donations ' That none but residing Canons were to have a share of the commons of the church.' . . . From the produce of his fishings at Perth, he contributed yearly, two stone weight of wax, for the lights of the great altar. . . . He died at Tibermuir on St. Cecilia's day, in the year 1249, and was buried in the old church, formerly the

Abbey Church of Dunkeld. . . . This is his epitaph: ' In this tomb, with his Father St. Colme, rests Galfred, the ornament and great support of the Church of Dunkeld.' "

Master Richard of Inverkeithing, great Chamberlain of Scotland, filled the See in 1250. When he died, his body was laid at Dunkeld, but his heart was placed in the north wall of the church at Inchcolme.

A famous Bishop was William Sinclair, uncle of William, Lord Bisset.

" He built the quire from the ground, in memorial of which he put a fluted cross on the last gavel, which to this day is used for the Arms of his family and name. He made a burial place for himself about the middle of the quire, near the stair of the Chapter house. There his body lies under a marble monument, and there was a handsome statue of him in alabaster. . . ."

While this clergyman resided at Achtertool, the Sheriff of Fife went with a body of 500 men against the English, who were laying waste the land. " The Sheriff fell back, the bishop armed himself, took horse with sixty of his people, meets the Sheriff and crys aloud, ' What madness is it in you to run away at this rate? ' The Sheriff replied, ' Because the English are more numerous and better soldiers than we are.' The Bishop said, ' if he got his due, the King would cause chop off his golden spurs, yet follow me and with assistance of St. Colme, whose lands they lay'd waste, we shall have our revenge.' He throws away his bishop's staff and grasps a spear. They did follow him, came up with the enemy, and happily obtained a great victory. There fell that day more than five hundred of the English, besides a number who by crowding into a barge overset it and were drowned."

The story makes one understand the love and respect which Robert the Bruce bore to this brave bishop. He always called him " My own Bishop," and directed letters to him in this form " To our Bishop."

Robert Cardney was another good Bishop to the Cathedral. He purchased the lands of " Mukleri," and out of the rents endowed a vicar at the altar of St. Ninian, which chapel he had built. He also built a strong castle for defence, glazed the windows of the choir at his own expense and bought a handsome mitre and bishop's staff. He was buried under a stone monument in St. Ninian's Chapel, this monument being afterwards removed to the Cathedral and is still there.

Bishop Thomas Lawder, preceptor to James II., was one of the greatest who adorned this See. He was sixty when appointed, and this venerable prelate had such an acquaintance with divinity, " that himself preached the faith to his parishioners."

The Bishops had been sadly troubled with freebooters in the district, lawless and fearless. Amongst them was Robert Reoch Macdonoquhy, a scourge to the church, for he repeatedly plundered the church lands of Little Dunkeld. Kemp, a wild robber of another type, had a stronghold on Stenton Rock, from which he descended to rob the unhappy pilgrims on their way with offerings to the Cathedral. There was besides that " archrobber Makbre, his sons and a gang," who extorted money and victuals from the bishop's tenants. Bishop Lawder imprisoned " one of that tribe which in Irish is named Clan Donoquhy, upon which Alexander Robertson, their chief, got together a band of ruffians, fell upon the bishop and threw a shower of arrows upon him at the very time in which he was, on Whitsunday, celebrating high Mass in the Cathedral, obliged him to give over the service and to take shelter behind some of the timber of the quire. . . . A complaint is entered of this outrage to the King, and Robertson had been put to death but for the interest of Lord Glammis, a great Court favourite, whose daughter he had married without a portion."

A Bishop's office was clearly no safe, easy sinecure in this " Gateway to the Highlands."

Bishop Lawder did much for Dunkeld Cathedral. He finished the aisle, glazed the windows, plastered the roof, built the south porch, beautifying it with fine images, founded the Steeple, and is credited with also founding the Chapter House, or at least adding to it. Having procured peace in the province, the Synod met in his own church; formerly the meetings had been held at Tulilum (Tullylumb), Perth, through fear of the Caterans. He also laid the foundations of a timber and stone bridge across the Tay.

He procured vestments of silk, silver candlesticks . . . a Cross in which there is a part of our Lord's Cross, and vessel for the Eucharist for the holy water, " all in silver." " There was over against the great Altar a piece of painting representing the 24 Miracles of St. Colme, and overhead of this, two statues of that saint; there were two pillars on which rested two angels, who held two candlesticks of fifteen branches . . . each suspended by a silken rope. He made a pillar for supporting the great wax lights." In addition to this, he promoted public worship by appointing chaplains and choristers, providing salaries for six singing boys and buying houses in Perth and Edinburgh for his successors. He died in the year 1481. His epitaph runs: " Christian people, pour out your joyful prayers for Thomas Lawder, your teacher. Do, O, Virgin, give him the name of Saint and let St. Thomas be placed near the good St. Colme in Heaven. He filled this See with unfading honour. The time was thirty years, but his good actions were past reckoning."

His successor, James Livingstoun, " was remarkable for his stature, and though he was rich, he was an affable, sweet-tempered, wise man."

The next was George Brown, the memory of whose piety and good works is still fragrant. He was a native of Dundee, his father being Town Treasurer there. The name is sometimes spelt Broun, but " w " was mostly used by translators of Myln's MS. He was involved in several lawsuits. owing to the perpetual encroachments of neighbouring nobles and others, who boldly seized the Church lands. Bishop Brown defended the Church possessions with unbroken courage and even added to them. His great desire was to travel betwixt the two palaces of Clunie and Dunkeld on his own ground. This he achieved, and could even ride between these places on four ways all his own ground. The forest and lands of Birnam and Logy he bought from the King, paying forty shillings yearly.

He erected altars and endowed them. He caused High Mass to be said at his own charge daily in honour of St.

Colme, who had preserved Dunkeld from the pestilence raging elsewhere in Scotland in the year 1500, and a curious account is given of his dealings with certain in Caputh afflicted with the disease. He first visited them and then " caused dip the bones of St. Colme in consecrated water and sent to them to drink. Many did drink and were cured. But there was one forward fellow among them who said, ' For what does the bishop send us water to drink? I could wish he had sent some of his best ale.' But he and thirty others who refused to drink the water died of the plague."

Bishop Brown also gave many ornaments to the church— silk copes, covers for the altar, images, portraits of saints drawn upon the wall all round, beautified the altars—and bought several bells. He built churches, houses, and began a bridge over the Tay. In 1510 he founded a benefaction which holds to this day, erecting St. George's Hospital for the purpose. This building was burnt in 1689, and small cottages were then built, but afterwards more substantial buildings were erected, part of which were sold. They occupy yet the corner of Cathedral Street, looking towards the Fountain and the Brae. The rents of these buildings were supposed to be applied to the support of seven old men in Dunkeld, called Bedesmen, who were originally each to have a free house and 2 pecks of oatmeal as well as a suit of white woollen cloth and ten shillings Scots yearly. At the Union of the Parishes of Auchtergaven and Logiebride in 1650, several curious items were brought up in Dunkeld Presbytery in connection with the Dunkeld Hospital of St. George and are narrated in Hunter's ' Diocese.'

The Bishop of Dunkeld in 1628 translated Mr. Alexander Anderson from Dunkeld and Dowally to Auchtergaven, which had before been worked conjointly with Logiebride. Separate stipends were given to each, and this created disturbance. The Minister of Logiebride as Prebendary of Fordeschaw and Master of the Hospital of Dunkeld had hitherto been burdened with a payment to the Bedesmen to be uplifted from the lands of Logiebride. The Bishop was indicted, among other counts, in 1638 for erecting " ane new paroshin and had given the rentes of ane hospitall to the minister's steepende, whereby all who belonged to the hospitall (if any did) behoved either for to begg or starve." Petitions for the Bedesmen were presented and Committees were appointed to visit the Hospital, the Synod coming to several findings. Part of the benefaction still remains and the Trust is now in the hands of the Sheriff of Perthshire, who appoints a delegate in Dunkeld.

Bishop Brown died in 1514 at Clunie Castle, whither he had retired, worn out with suffering and sorrow over Flodden. Canon Myln was present at his death, of which he gives a circumstantial and affecting account.

There is a window in the ruined Nave to this good Bishop's memory. A saying of his sheds a light on his generosity and upright disposition; severe in discipline, he yet refused to apply to his own use fines of offenders, and often said, " The oil of the wicked will never make my head to shine."

Several short descriptions are given of the various officials during his charge. Mr. Walter Brown took care that " no low wit or scandal were admitted to his table." Mr. Thomas Greig's " temper was somewhat passionate, but after all, he was a kind-hearted man." ...

Mr. James Lawder was " a virtuous, modest, decent young man . . . much beloved for being so obliging to his superiors." Mr. Thomas Bettoun " had great execution in musick and had a voice he could tune to any key. . . He honours the virgin . . . and hates sloth. His furniture is handsome, and he has a turn for gardening."

Mr. John Martyne, John Lesly and William Scherar were three priests born in Dunkeld who had " great knowledge of musick and from their youth have been in use to direct the quire." Canon Myln closes with an account of the stormy entry of Gavin Douglas to the Diocese of Dunkeld.

CHAPTER V.

Gavin Douglas, the Poet-Bishop of Dunkeld.

UNDOUBTEDLY the most illustrious of the Dunkeld Bishops was Gavin Douglas, son of that stern Douglas nicknamed Bell the Cat, who thanked " St. Bothan, son of mine, save Gavin, ne'er could pen a line."

More than two hundred years ago Allan Ramsay, the poet, boasted proudly of Douglas when he wrote—

> " In the lear'd days o' Gawn Dunkell
> Our country then a tale could tell,
> Europe had nane mair snack or snell
>   At verse or prose,"

And a century later, Sir Walter Scott thus describes the Poet-Bishop in " Marmion "—

> " A Bishop by the altar stood,
> A noble lord of Douglas' blood,
> With mitre sheen and racquet white
> Yet showed his meek and thoughtful eye,
> But little pride of prelacy,
> More pleased that in a barbarous age
> He gave rude Scotland Virgil's page,
> Than that beneath his rule he held
> The bishopric of fair Dunkeld."

Douglas was the pioneer of classic culture in Scotland, and was the author of the first translation in the vernacular of a Latin classic published in Britain. Before succeeding to the Bishopric he was the Provost of St. Giles, Edinburgh, and Rector of Hawick.

Scottish patriots should be proud of Gavin Douglas. He made it a boast that he " speke in the auld braid Scots " and that he " kepand na Soudron bot ouir awin langage." At that period it was reckoned the mark of a traitor to " knapp Soudron " (Anglice, know Southern or English speech.)

The language, therefore, in which he wrote accounts largely for the neglect of his poetry. It is more obscure than that of Dunbar, but the ringing, manly vigour of the Bishop's lines, the glowing ardour of his description, and the thrilling sweetness with which he lingers over soft summer beauties, more than repays the student who reads, though with glossary in hand.

His translation of Virgil is highly praised, and rightly, so it is unfortunate that his patriotism should have prevented this scholarly work from achieving more popularity. There is a copy in the Mackintosh Library in Dunkeld.

The Prologues to the twelve books of the Æneid consist of original and charming descriptions of the seasons.   So vivid is the portrayal of

" the firmament ourecast with cludes black,
     the mountane toppes fleked with snaw,
     the law vales floderit all with spate "

that we easily envisage the black clouds, the white mountain tops, and hear the rattle of the " scharp hailstanes hoppand on the thak " and the roar of " ryvers running red on spate."

Who, having experienced the rigours of a Scottish winter, can fail to sympathise with the poet when he tells how he,

" bounit (came nearer) to the fire, chevarand of cald,
     the sessound was sae snell "?

Then in the " wynter cald " he goes to bed all "warped up," but nevertheless lies awake listening to

" the eerie noises of the darksome night "

Not the least being the " claking of the wyld geis " as they glide high in the air over the city, or the " hooting owl, that hornyt bird, laithly of form."

Dwellers near the Cathedral of which he became Bishop can heartily endorse his objection to the hideous clamour of night when these " hornyt birds " wail their secrets to each other within the roofless walls and behind the gaping windows. This is his song of winter.   But with a shout of glee he welcomes May—

"Welcum, the lord of licht and lampe of day,
  Welcum, fosterare of tender herbes green,
  Welcum, the birdis beild apoun the brere,
  Welcum, depaynter of the blomyt medis."
With keen delight he listened to the " bemying of the bees
and the birds sang in warblis dulce of hevinle armonys."
Nor did the tiniest flower escape the notice of this keen ob-
server of Nature—
  " The dasy did onbrede (unbraid) her crownel smale,
    the heavinle lyllis with looker and toppes quhyte, (curling
      white tops),
    distilled halesome hony droppis."
Other works testify still more to his erudition. " King
Hart " is an allogorical poem, in which the life of man is
traced from " Youth so fair, so fresh, so likely to endure,
blyth as byrd in summer scheme " to " Age when Strength
yields to Decrepitude, whose loathly limbs all crooked were
with eld."

The Palace of Honour is another allegory abounding in
many charming passages, but overloaded with classical
allusions, a fault common to the age.

Here the author relates a dream. In it he sees travellers
of all sorts—Mars, Minerva, the Muses, Wood Nymphs—
wending their way to the Palace of Honour. He joins them
and reaches the throne of Venus. Behind this throne is a
magic mirror. Over its polished surface flit the shadows of
famous personages of the misty past; amongst them the
mighty Ossianic heroes, Fingal and Fin Mac Cowl.

Venus hands Douglas a copy of Virgil, with a command
to translate it into his native tongue, which command he
afterwards obeyed. He then set out to visit a delightful
garden where the Muses gathered flowers of poesy and the
trees bore precious stones. Surrounding this Paradise was a
deep ditch, spanned by a narrow bridge representing the
ceremony of marriage. The passage across was too precarious
for the dreamer. He slipped, fell—and awoke!

The Queen Regent was at Perth when Bishop Brown
died. She wished Douglas to be appointed to the vacant See,
and Pope Leo the Tenth acquiesced.

Learned, gentle and pious, however, as Gavin Douglas was acclaimed, his nomination gave dire offence. Already the Chapter in Dunkeld had elected Andrew Stewart, brother to the Earl of Atholl. In his quaint style, Canon Myln tells of this election, "John, Earl of Athol, the son of Earl John, brother to King James II., called the Canons and requested of them to make choice of his brother Andrew, Prebendary of Craigyne, and in the meantime to put the episcopal palace in his possession. As some of the canons were his relations and others were afraid for themselves and effects, therefore they without delay agreed to grant all that was desired. . . The affair went the more easily that the Earl was very powerful and could defend everybody belonging to the church from plunderers of every kind."

It was not to be supposed, therefore, that the Earl of Atholl and his brother would submit without a struggle to the nomination of another, and that other a member of the rival, influential House of Douglas. The Earl and his brother took the high patriotic stand and quoted an ancient Scottish law, seldom enforced, which forbade the using of outside influence. They averred that Douglas had done this through the Queen Regent, who had used the interest of the English King to procure the Papal nomination, and declared him a traitor. Douglas was therefore tried on the charge of treason, found guilty and condemned to imprisonment. For more than a year he languished a prisoner in the Castles of Edinburgh, St. Andrews and Dunbar.

The Queen Regent (widow of James IV.) was very angry at this flouting of her authority. She had married the Earl of Angus, nephew of Gavin Douglas, shortly after the death of the King, a marriage by which our Royal family are descended through Darnley. She refused to yield, and succeeded finally in obtaining the freedom and recognition of her nominee.

Douglas was then consecrated at Glasgow, but before him was still a stormy passage. Myln's account of his ordination confirms this—

"After his consecration he first visited St. Andrews on Michaelmas Week, then the Church of Dunkeld. The first night he was very affectionately received by clergy and laity, who all praised God for so noble, so learned, so worthy a Bishop. He published the bulls at the great Altar, gave his blessing, and lodged at the dean's house, as he had no access to the palace, which, with the steeple, Andrew Stewart's servants held out for him, refusing to deliver them, alleging they did all by authority of the regent (Duke of Albany). On this account he was forced to have the service of God performed in the Dean's House. To this place he called the Canons, and it was with their whole heart they yielded him homage."

This Dean's house, last of old Dunkeld, is still standing and inhabited. It is one of a block near the Cathedral gate, which survived the disastrous fire at the Battle of Dunkeld in 1689, and is easily recognised by the massive door. In recent alterations, efforts were made to preserve the ancient character of the house. A subterranean passage was said to have been discovered near, probably one leading to the Cathedral.

After dinner, Bishop Douglas consulted the gentlemen and clergy who were present as to the course he ought to follow. In the midst of those consultations, information was received that Andrew Stewart was in arms, and a shower of cannon shot from Steeple and Palace also alarmed them. People of rank hurried to the Bishop's defence; notice was sent to friends and " next day there came such crowds from Montross, from the low parts of Fife and the country roundabout that the City could scarce hold them. But for all their number the Prebendary of Alith had laid up such abundance of everything that there was room and provisions for all the men and also for their horses."

Andrew Stewart, thus rendered unable to relieve his retainers in palace and steeple, retired to the woods. Excommunication was threatened by the Bishop, with the result that the steeple was placed in his possession. Afterwards there were mutual accusations at Court, but a compromise being effected, Stewart retained the rents he had collected and Douglas was settled in the diocese.

The Bishop then gave himself over to good works in the bishopric. The bridge across the Tay which his predecessor

began he continued, but this bridge vanished long ago. He
maintained peace in his province, and also endeavoured to
play the part of peacemaker elsewhere.

In 1520 several nobles, nominally headed by the Earl of
Arran, but instigated by the Primate, Cardinal Beaton, met
in Edinburgh, their real object being the humbling of the
Earl of Angus. Douglas was present, and in vain endeavoured
to bring matters to a peaceable conclusion. Turning to
Beaton, he reminded him that he was a servant of the Prince
of Peace and implored him to use his influence for peace.

" It may not be," was the proud prelate's answer.
" Angus is too insolent. As for Arran's designs, upon my
conscience, I know nothing!"

While speaking, Beaton struck his breast as if in emphasis,
forgetting that beneath his princely garb he wore a steel
hauberk. The steel rattled loudly.

The answer of Douglas shows he had a ready wit. " Ah,
my lord," said he, " I perceive your conscience is not sound,
for I hear it clatter!"

The affair ended in a sharp skirmish, during which
Douglas retired to pray. Angus was victorious, and only the
intervention of the Bishop saved Beaton as he sheltered
behind the Altar of Blackfriars Church.

The times were troublous, and such broils embittered
the life and banished the muse of the Poet-Bishop. His
enemies became more and more powerful. Even the revenues
of Dunkeld Cathedral were sequestrated, and at last Douglas
formed the project of visiting Rome in the hope that there
he might plead his cause and receive help. He reached
London, and, lingering there, he died of the plague in 1522.

There is no memorial in Dunkeld to mark its connection
with this talented bishop, save a stone bearing the Arms of
the Douglases, found amongst rubbish, and defaced. For a
time it occupied a place over a former Royal School building,
but is now in the Cathedral, where are also to be seen
armorial bearings of the various bishops and heritors in the
district.

In Perth, a line to the Bishop's memory is recorded on
the panel commemorating the site of the Palace of the Dunkeld
Bishops. Such a panel might fitly be placed on the Dean's
house where the ordination of Douglas took place.

CHAPTER. VI.

"And here, no doubt, too, wondrous Crichton strayed
That prodigy whom bounteous Nature made
A sage in childhood."

—*Millar.*

The Admirable Crichton.

BISHOP DOUGLAS was succeeded by Bishop George Chrichton, the very antithesis of his poetic and learned predecessor, for it is related of him that he thanked God he knew neither the Old nor New Testaments, yet had prospered well enough. He made this boast when addressing Dean Thomas Forrest, one of the vicars, who was afterwards burnt as a heretic on the Castle Hill, Edinburgh. "Dean Thomas," said he, "if you leave not these phantasies, you will repent it when you cannot mend it."

In his "Sketches of Scottish History," the Revd. Thomas McCrie alludes to this speech, and says, "There arose a proverb which was commonly applied in Scotland for many years after to persons who were grossly ignorant, 'Ye are like the Bishop of Dunkeld, that kent neither new law nor auld.'"

It is also recorded of this Bishop that he was "a man nobly disposed and a great housekeeper, but in matters of his calling not very skilled. In questions of his religion, which, in his time, was severely agitated, he loved to have things calmly carried, but his counsel took little place."

Such a bishop would not be in sympathy with the Reformation of the Church; he did not vex his soul about matters of doctrine, but he did wish to prevent the spoliators from enjoying the revenue of those Church lands which his predecessors had worthily and laboriously added to the Barony

D

of Dunkeld.   He saw a change coming and made a futile effort
to preserve Clunie lands for the Cathedral.   He died ere the
Reformation culminated, and his nephew Robert succeeded to
the See in 1559.

Through the instrumentality of Bishop Crichton, Clunie
Castle and the adjoining lands were conveyed to a kinsman,
Robert Crichton of Eliock, in Nithdale, who was also Lord
Advocate of Scotland.   There was a proviso, however, that
possession of the property should not be taken without his
leave and that occupants should remove themselves within
forty days if required.   The Reformation made this proviso
valueless, and there is no record of the property ever revert-
ing to the Church.   The Crichtons retained possession, as did
many other nobles in various parts of Scotland.

This action of Bishop Crichton brought the " Admirable
Crichton," claimed as " the greatest prodigy the world ever
saw," to Clunie Castle.   He followed in the footsteps of
Bishop Douglas, winning Continental fame as a scholar and
worthily upholding Scotland's lamp of learning in dark days.
To the Poet Bishop he seemed more akin than to the bishop
who had boasted of lack of learning.   Robert Crichton with
his family took up residence at Clunie in 1562.   His wife
was Elizabeth Stewart, and through her the Admirable
Crichton could claim Royal descent.   Several places claim
the honour of being the birthplace of James Crichton, the
wonderful scholar, Clunie and Nithsdale amongst the rest.
The date of his birth is generally accepted as 1560, so it is
unlikely that if the family did not reside in Clunie until 1562
he would be born there, but was brought as a young infant to
the Castle, which is still in good preservation, though un-
inhabited, and now a favourite place for picnic parties.

It is built on a small islet in Clunie Loch, which was once
a stronghold of a gang of robbers who terrorised and robbed
the Church tenants.   To prevent this, Bishop Brown built
a house and chapel on the islet, only preserving the vault of
the former Castle.   It was his favourite residence; here the
good Bishop retired for meditation, and here he died.   The
Castle was known as " The Key of the See of Dunkeld."

James Crichton's boyhood was certainly spent at Clunie.

Here, as the poet says, he strayed " o'er that wooded hill,"
or rejoiced as his glance wandered o'er the broad lake's bosom,
where the green islet, his boyhood's home, rested. It is not
unlikely that he visited Dunkeld, where his kinsmen had been
bishops, though their glory and that of the Cathedral were
sadly diminished. It is even probable that he might have
received early tuition there, for there was a Grammar
School in the Church of St. George in the Cathedral and the
Royal School in Dunkeld was founded in 1567. He had some
schooling in Perth, and then went to St. Andrews.

He had a wonderful career, about which there has been
much controversy. Tytler, the historian of Scotland, in his
" Life of Crichton," follows the account of the various Continental scholars, who lauded the youthful Scot as a prodigy
of learning.

This youth of " very wonderful genius," as Scaliger, the
famous Continental scholar, afterwards said of him, took his
degree of B.A. at the age of twelve, and two years after, that
of M.A. He is actually said to have acquired ten languages
besides his own, and was able to write and speak them fluently.
He became a fellow student of James VI., under the tutorship
of George Buchanan. Afterwards he set out on the grand
tour through Europe and there displayed his erudition and
eloquence after the manner of the times. In Paris he issued
a challenge to all " savants " in the city, offering to dispute
with any on literature, science and art, in prose or verse, in
the following languages, " Hebrew, Syriac, Arabic, Greek,
Latin, Spanish, French, English, Italian, Dutch, Flemish or
Sclavonic." There was a great meeting. Over 3000 people
were present, including Church dignitaries, and he disputed
with over fifty learned men, who plied him with questions of
every kind, all of which he answered. From nine in the
morning until six at night the discussion went on, and at the
close he was addressed as " L'Admirable Crichton " and
presented with a purse of gold and a diamond ring.

Not only was he a marvel in learning, he was an expert
swordsman, and worsted another of European fame hitherto
undefeated. " L'Admirable Crichton " was also claimed as a
model of manly beauty, a genius in music, the possessor of a

fine voice. In the great cities of the Continent, Rome, Venice, Paris, Padua, men flocked to listen to his discourses on philosophy. Copies of his verses were eagerly circulated; a few are still extant; the Latin Ode to Massa, said to be a lyric of uncommon beauty, is full of classic elegance.

His career soon closed. Mystery surrounds his death. It is generally believed that he was assassinated by his pupil, the Prince of Mantua, either by his own hand or by his order.

Joseph Justus Scaliger, reputed the greatest scholar of his times, while admitting that he was a very wonderful genius, qualifies his statement by saying that he was " more worthy of admiration than esteem." Still, even great scholars are prone to jealousy, and Scaliger may have felt a twinge of it when listening to Crichton's praises. Scaliger, too, came to England, and confesses that he did not like the people, but it is curious to find that he drew a distinction between the English and the Scots, viewing the latter more favourably and according hearty praise to Scottish ballads.

Crichton had served in the French Army, and although his distinction in Rome as a disputant is sometimes denied, he certainly achieved distinction in Padua. Aldus Manutius, grandson of the founder of the Aldine Press, took him under his patronage and lauded him to the skies. Another James Crichton was on the Continent at the same time, and the two have sometimes been confused. Sir Thomas Urquhart wrote in 1652 an extravagant eulogy on " L'Admirable Crichton," hailing him as the " Discovery of a most exquisite Jewel."

His advent and his passing at the early age of 22 certainly created some stir in Continental circles whatever might be the manner of his life or death—

> " The talented, the brave, the young
> The gay, the beautiful,—so praised, so sung,
> So loved, so gifted, and so early lost—
> A comet blazing mid a countless host
> Of dimmer stars—Scarce wondered at when gone
> Leaving no trace behind but that it shone,
> And was admired !"
>
> —D. Millar

CHAPTER VII.

Dunkeld Cathedral: Its Destruction.

ROBERT CRICHTON was the last of the long line of Roman Catholic Bishops, and the destruction of Dunkeld's sacred pile took place in his time, when the full tide of the Reformation swept over the land, bringing down the princely prelates and laying waste many a fair pile. The Church lands which the Bishops had acquired were snatched from their rule, and so low did the revenues of Dunkeld, amongst others, become that the King had to make a gift of a hundred pounds to the incumbent in 1689.

The Cathedral, which each Bishop, in love and pride, had striven to adorn and beautify, exterior and interior, owes its destruction to the misguided zeal and frenzied recklessness of a number of the Reformers. The building, as has been shown from its situation in a natural opening in that great mountain barrier of the Grampians, had been subjected to many fierce attacks. The mountain caterans who scorned priestly censure descended on the rich domain and plundered fearlessly, speeding back laden with booty to their own hills. Turbulent chiefs and their vassals stormed on more than one occasion the Episcopal Palace and the strong Castle built for defence; at the celebration of the Festival of Pentecost they had not hesitated to touch the sacred building itself. The Bishop of that day had to climb the rafters to escape the unwelcome attentions of the Clan Donachie, and the famous Bishop Douglas was, as has been related, installed in the midst of a shower of shot. Neighbouring lairds are said to have coveted the rich flocks and lands of the See, and involved several of the bishops in lawsuits. The Dunkeld clergy were thus forced to keep a wary watch on their northern enemies, and that they gave the benefit of their observations to their southern brethren is a matter of history. Sir Walter Scott takes note of this kindness, which was also an act of policy, in the " Fair Maid of Perth." The Prior of the Dominicans in Perth warns King Robert and his Councillors " that the last advice from the brethren in Dunkeld informs them that the Clan Chattan and Quhele are ready to break out into a more formidable warfare and that the Fiery Cross was flitting like a meteor in every direction." This advice led to the famous Clan Battle of 1396 in Perth.

Yet the Cathedral survived these barbarous attacks and grew in beauty, a noble structure to cherish and to be proud of. It was unfortunately reserved for the leaders of the Reformation to bring ruin upon it, and to make its walls desolate, naked and bare,

> " As if they waged an architectural war,
> To banish art, and beauty's self to mar."

The Cathedral thus remains an unedifying witness to the violence of man's bigotry and passions, urged on by mad, unreasoning zeal. It is well, however, to note that the leaders who issued the order which led to the destruction of the building did not intend the ruin to be so complete.

The Order was issued in 1560 by the Privy Council of Scotland, and runs as follows :—

" Order of the Privy Council of Scotland for demolishing the altars and imagery of the Cathedral:

" To our traist friendis, the Lairds of Arntilly and Kinvaid.

" Traist friendis, after maist harty commendacion we pray you faill not to pass incontinent to the Kyrk of Dunkeld and tak doun the haill images thereof, and bring furth to the kirk-yayrd, and burn them oppenly, and siclyk cast doun the altaris and purge the kirk of all kind of monuments of idolatrye. And this ze faill not to do, as ze will do us singular empleseur, and so committis you to the protection of God.

" From Edinburgh, the XII. day of August, 1560. Faill not, bot ye tak guid heyd that neither the desks, windocks, nor durris, be in ony weys hurt or broken—eyther glassin wark or iron wark.

(Signed) " AR. ERGYLL
" JAMES STEWART.
" RUTHVEN."

It will be observed that this Order was, in many important respects, wantonly disobeyed. Care was not taken of the glass or iron work. Windows were smashed, doors torn off their hinges, monuments defaced and mutilated, while the building was unroofed. Nor was this wanton and wicked destruction done by an ignorant and careless mob. The orders were sent to two men of position, lairds of neighbouring estates, and one of the chief leaders besides in the wholesale destruction which went on, is said to have been the Laird of Cardney, a member of the same family as one of the founders, Bishop Cardney. Shame might have stayed his hands, or pride in his illustrious kinsman, whose tomb is still to be seen within the ruined Nave. The family tomb of this Laird is also within its walls. It may be probable that these men knew what nobles such as Argyll and Ruthven really desired and proceeded accordingly.

The Cathedral never recovered its glory, nor the Bishops their power. The ornaments of gold and silver work, the silk vestments, the paintings, all of which so graphically described by Canon Myln, have vanished and none know whither. Not even the relics of St. Columba remain.

In 1571 the See of Dunkeld was declared to be void through process of forfeiture against Robert Crichton, sometime bishop thereof. Acts of Assembly in 1586 and 1593 appointed Dunkeld the Seat of Presbyterial Meetings, but during the next century the history of the church is mainly the record of the conflict between Presbyterianism and Episcopacy. In 1609, by Act of Parliament, Episcopal Jurisdiction was restored, and by another Act in 1617 " Anent the Restitutioun of Chapteris," the Bishop of Dunkeld was appointed one of the chapter for the election of the Archbishop of St. Andrews, and Vicar General for convening the electors.

In a valuable work entitled " The Diocese and Presbytery of Dunkeld, 1660-1689," by the Rev. John Hunter, B.D., Minister of the Parish of Rattray, who died in 1915, there is much reliable information, compiled as it was from Ecclesiastical Registers and other Records. In the Introduction it is pointed out " that the references to the Cathedral fabric are disappointingly meagre," although there are many details of historical value regarding the Chapter. Here it is also remarked that during the various changes from the Reformation to the final abolition of Prelacy in 1690 few of the Presbyterian Ministers in this part of Scotland refused compliance when Episcopacy was abolished or restored. They were not re-ordained when a Bishop was set over them, and even the bishop himself in 1662 was consecrated without being re-ordained (as all the Scottish Bishops had been in 1610), There was little striking change in public worship, and scarcely any trace of sympathy with the Covenanters or signs of persecution in the district. Probably Dunkeld lay too close to the Highland border to be largely interested in the beliefs and doings of the southern part of Scotland.

Dunkeld Cathedral and its Bishops were of small importance during this period. Archbishop Spottiswood in his " History of the Church " gives a List of seven Bishops of Dunkeld after the Reformation, and three more are recorded in the Register of the Great Seal. These Bishops did not reside at Dunkeld but at Meigle, the reason being that the living at Meigle was attached to the Bishopric in 1607, in order to augment the stipend at Dunkeld, the gross rental being so poor. In Scots money it was declared after the Revolution to be only £1810 17s. 10d. (Scots). Therefore the Bishops resided in the Manse at Meigle, with one exception, George Haliburton, who lived at Perth.

One of these Bishops, Peter Rollock, granted a Charter in 1605 with advice and consent of the Dean and Chapter of Dunkeld, which gave many privileges to the City of Dunkeld, citizens and indwellers thereof. This Charter was ratified and confirmed by Charles I. in 1641.

Another Bishop, Henry Guthrie, is remembered by his " Memoirs," which give many interesting details of the period, and then there was that Bishop, Dr Andrew Bruce, who was bold enough to oppose the repeal of the penal statutes against Roman Catholics in the Scots Parliament of 1686. The King was angry and deprived him of his office, forbidding rents or revenues to be paid to him. When the Revolution of 1689 was impending, James endeavoured to conciliate the Scottish Bishops, and recommended Andrew, late Bishop of Dunkeld, to the vacant See of Orkney. To this charge he was elected, only to lose it in the Revolution.

Little was done during these years of conflict to repair or beautify the Cathedral. In 1600, Stewart of Ladywell repaired and re-roofed the Choir for public worship. This family held for a time the office of Commissary of Dunkeld, and one of its members, John Stewart, became, unfortunately for himself, involved in the disputes between Montrose and Argyle. He paid the penalty, being executed for treason in 1641. There is a Memorial Tablet to the family, in Dunkeld Cathedral, as also their Coat of Arms on the wall.

In the Presbyterial Records, too, there are numerous complaints of the spoliation endured at the hands of the Irish levies brought in by Alaster Macdonald of Colketto, when he joined the gallant Montrose and the Athollmen. It is recorded in the Registers that the brethren of Dunkeld were absent from the Synod meetings in Perth because of the approach of the " crewel and bloody armies of Irish rebels under the Marquis of Montrose," and ministers of the various congregations also complained bitterly of being despoiled of their goods and forced to flee from their manses.

While some ministers in the Dunkeld Presbytery were thus prevented from attending meetings " by the crewel rebels," several, on the other hand, were rebuked by the Synod for trafficking with Montrose. Mr George Haliburton, afterwards Bishop of Dunkeld, was sharply reprimanded. He was accused of " eating and drinking with Montrose and saying ' Grace ' at his table."

Montrose entered and re-entered Dunkeld during his meteoric career when winning battles for Charles I., making it his headquarters on several occasions. To achieve his project of carrying Dundee by storm, he left Dunkeld at daybreak and on the following day succeeded in his enterprise. He hovered in and near Dunkeld whilst waiting for reinforcements before marching south after the Alford victory in 1645; the Atholemen joining him and doing yeomen service in his famous Highland campaign.

In 1689 the Cathedral received another blow. Its tower and walls were used as places of defence during the Battle of Dunkeld and bear marks to this day of the fierce struggle which then took place.

CHAPTER VIII.

The Battle of Dunkeld.

PICTS, Scots and Danes, prelates, nobles and caterans, had all warred round Dunkeld, but the little city had won through in spite of repeated conflagrations and sackings. It was, however, now to receive its heaviest blow. It had its share of trouble during the war between King and Commonwealth; it had rejoiced, with others, in the Restoration of 1660, but the completion of the Revolution, which banished King James and placed William and Mary on the throne, reduced it to ashes. The Marquess of Atholl had been a warm supporter of the House of Stewart during these troubles. Montrose had always received a welcome at Blair, but a change occurred. James VII. with his Roman Catholic proclivities offended many warm supporters of the Stewarts, and allegiance was transferred to William of Orange. Amongst them was the Atholl family, but Blair Castle was seized by the Jacobites and garrisoned for James. Lord Murray, son of the Marquess, collected a force at Dunkeld and set out to relieve the Castle, retreating when news came that Viscount Dundee (or Dundie, as old papers have it) was on the march to Blair. This attempt to gain possession of Blair by the Jacobites sent General Mackay, Commander of William's forces, to Killiecrankie. Marching first from Perth to Dunkeld, he sent forward from the latter place fusileers to reinforce the Atholl men at Killiecrankie and then followed them early next morning. The armies met and Mackay was defeated, but Dundee fell in the moment of victory. His loss ruined the cause of James, though his army did not wholly melt away until the Battle of Dunkeld was fought, a month later. This Battle or Siege is a memorable one in the annals of Scottish History, for it practically closed a Civil War and completed the Revolution.

In Browne's History of the Highlands is a stirring account of this battle. If short, it was a fierce and savage affair, ending in the complete destruction of the town of Dunkeld, with the exception of three houses. The conflict took place between the Cameronians and the remnants of Dundee's army, raging furiously within the town, round the Cathedral and the house of the Marquess of Atholl. The Cameronians were a band of religious enthusiasts, followers of Richard Cameron, the Martyr. Hungering for vengeance on their persecutors, they answered the call of the Scottish Convention for aid in 1689. Edinburgh Castle was holding out for King James; it surrendered to them. Afterwards the Cameronians were sent to Perthshire, their objective being Dunkeld.

General Mackay remonstrated with the Scottish Privy Council on this move, pointing out that there was bitter animosity between them and the Jacobites. In Dunkeld they would be exposed to much hostility with very small chance of defence, surrounded by unfriendly clansmen, many of whom were still under arms, led by General Cannon, Dundee's successor.

Mackay's remonstrance was in vain. The troops were sent off under the leadership of Lieut.-Colonel Cleland, who, although but 28 years old, had already seen much service. At 18, he had been a Captain in the Covenanting forces, had fought both at Bothwell Brig and Drumclog, been outlawed and lurked a fugitive in the wilds of Ayrshire and Clydesdale. An accomplished poet besides, he had written a stinging satire on the "Highland Host." It was therefore far from likely that he and his regiment would be severely left alone by the fiery Highlanders.

Mackay's opinion proved correct. On Saturday, the 17th August, 1689, the Cameronians, 1200 all told, reached Dunkeld. Next morning they saw that the atmosphere was hostile and entrenched themselves in the enclosures of Dunkeld House, besides placing a detachment in the Cathedral Tower, strict Sabbatarians though they were.

At intervals small parties of men appeared on the hills overlooking the town. At 4 o'clock a gathering of several hundreds drew up on the hill to the north. A messenger, who bore a halbert surmounted with a white cloth as flag of truce, was sent with a letter to Colonel Cleland couched in the following terms:—" We, the gentlemen assembled, being informed that ye intend to burn the town, desire whether ye come for peace or war, and to certify you that if ye burn any one house, we will destroy you."

Cleland refused to leave the town, but sent for reinforcements, as he heard the Fiery Cross was being sent round the hills, and he might therefore expect a still larger gathering of opponents.

In response to his appeal, Lord Cardross arrived with several cavalry troops, and a few slight engagements occurred outside the town with the clansmen. To the astonishment, however, of Lord Cardross and Cleland, an imperative order was received from Colonel Ramsay, Commander in Perth, requesting Cardross to return immediately with his troops. Cleland uttered strong objections, but the other conceived it his duty to obey orders and returned, though reluctantly, to Perth. On Wednesday, the 21st August, it was only too apparent that the Fiery Cross had been successful and that the whole Highland army had arrived. It was drawn up on the hills in order of battle.

The Cameronians could not retreat; they were surrounded. They could not surrender, for they had never shown mercy, and need expect none. Nothing remained but to fight.

Cleland skilfully posted parties in the Cathedral Steeple, and in the town. Throwing up ditches for a line of defence, he placed others behind the adjoining gardens and park, all having been done before seven in the morning.

General Cannon, leader of the opposing forces, despatched two troops to guard the ford on the Tay near the Cathedral in an endeavour to prevent the Cameronians escaping by water, whilst other troops were placed at the opposite end of the town.

The Jacobites were at first successful, forcing outposts and entering at four different points so that the battle raged throughout the town. At the Cross, Lieutenant Stewart, on the Cameronian side, held a barricade until he was killed, a heavy fire meanwhile being kept up from the Cathedral (which still shows bullet marks in the eastern gable).

The Highlanders crowded into all the neighbouring houses and poured a galling fire on the Cathedral and Atholl Mansion House garrisons. The struggle was one of the utmost ferocity, claymores and muskets, pikes and halberts exacted and paid heavy toll, so heavy indeed that it was suspected the Evil One himself was giving assistance. This suspicion is touched upon by Sir Walter Scott in "Guy Mannering." The novelist says that the Laird of Ellangowan, "Donohoe Bertram," took his grey gelding and joined Clavers at Killiecrankie. At the skirmish of Dunkeld, 1689, he was shot dead by a Cameronian with a silver button (being supposed to be proof from the Evil One against lead and steel), and his grave is still called "The Wicked Laird's Lair."

Soon a heavy loss was sustained by the Cameronians. Their leader fell, wounded in two places, as he was encouraging his men "to do their duty and fear not." Bleeding, he bravely endeavoured to crawl out of sight into Dunkeld House, in the hope that his men might not observe him and thus be dispirited. The effort was not successful and he expired in the street, his body afterwards being laid to rest near the Tower, where a simple stone with date and name marks the spot.

Major Henderson took his place, only to be shot down in a few minutes. He was succeeded by Captain Munro, who dislodged the Highlanders by setting fire to the town. He sent pikemen with blazing faggots upon the points of their pikes, which they thrust into the thatched roofs of the houses occupied by the enemy. Thence ensued a terrible scene, and on that summer day, with the heather abloom on the surrounding hills, the unfortunate citizens of the little town nestling under the shadow of a building dedicated to the Prince of Peace, tasted to the full the horrors of war.

The following is quoted from Browne's "History of the Highlands":—"The whole town was in a conflagration, and the scene which it now presented was one of the most heart-rending description. The din of war was no longer heard, but a more terrific sound had succeeded, from the wild shrieks and accents of despair which issued from the dense mass of smoke and flame which enveloped the unfortunate sufferers. The pikemen had locked the doors of such of the houses as had keys standing in them and the unhappy intruders, being thus cut off from escape, perished in the flames. No less than sixteen Highlanders were burnt to death in one house. With the exception of three houses, possessed by the Cameronians, the whole town was consumed.'' This sharp conflict had lasted for four hours altogether. The Cameronians were reduced nearly to their last flask of powder and were stripping lead from the roof of Dunkeld House, to cut into slugs, when the Highlanders retired, their ammunition done and no shelter obtainable in the ruined town. General Cannon attempted to persuade them to renew the attack, but they declined, saying '' they were ready to fight with men, but would not again encounter devils ! '' The same idea is expressed in a Jacobite ballad, which thus concludes :—

> "You fought like devils, your only rivals,
>   When you were at Dunkeld, boys."

After hurling defiance at their retreating foes, the Cameronians showed their joy by singing Psalms. Macaulay says, '' Then the drums struck up, the victorious Puritans threw their caps in the air, raised with one voice a psalm of triumph and thanksgiving and waved their colours—colours which were on that day unfurled for the first time in the face of an enemy.''

History does not record if the unfortunate inhabitants took part in the rejoicings. Probably not, as they were burnt out and forced to shelter in the Cathedral. For them only remained ruined homes. In the '' Life of Colonel Blackadder '' there is also a stirring account of this encounter between Highlanders and Cameronians, sworn foes.

Thus ended one of the most disastrous days Dunkeld has seen. A new Dunkeld arose from the ruins, but different in aspect and different in position. It may even be considered that the town never regained its former prestige.

CHAPTER IX.

Historic Events After 1689.

THE little city, though thus reduced to ashes, rose again and played its part in various recorded historical events. The Earl of Mar, after raising the Standard for King James in 1715 at Braemar, also formed four regiments of Athollmen at Dunkeld, and many suffered for the support they gave to the Stewart cause in '15. General Wade helped to suppress this Rising, but he is remembered chiefly by the military roads he constructed in the Highlands. One of his roads linked up Fort George with Dunkeld, and there are yet many traces of his work in the district. His roads connected various towns in the Highlands with Perth and Stirling, and Dunkeld was one of those thus favoured. The great North Road passed through it on to Inverness, although the first three miles of the present road is not the one constructed by him about 1739. Wade's road began opposite Inver at the West Ferry, running along by the river side until it reached the higher ground two miles from Dowally. From that point his road is still in use but altered and improved, for it was so rough that one of the Dukes of Atholl is said to have taken twelve hours to drive from Dunkeld to Blair Atholl. The General did not build his projected bridge over the Tay at Dunkeld, showing his resentment at an imagined affront he received from the Duke by building the bridge at Aberfeldy instead. Other bridges of his, though of less importance, are in the neighbourhood. One at Ballinloan, in Strathbraan, forms a picturesque feature in the landscape; another at Dalguise, near the Tay, is in ruins.

The '45 brought trouble and tribulation to Dunkeld. In September, 1745, the " Bonnie Prince Charlie " of Jacobite

ballads was entertained in Dunkeld House by the Marquis
of Tullibardine, second son of the first Duke of Atholl.
Another son, Lord George Murray, of whom an old ballad
sings—

> " He's the flow'r o' Glenisla
> An' the darlin' o' Dunkel',"

recruited actively for the Prince, becoming the Lieut.-General
of the Jacobite Forces. The Chevalier was proclaimed King
at the Market Cross, and Prince Charles also proclaimed as
Regent for his father by Lord Nairne and Cameron of Lochiel,
who had come to Dunkeld some days before. This Cross stood
where the Fountain now stands, but was removed about 1800.
It was a round stone pillar on which were four balls supporting
a pyramidal top. It was 20 feet high and to it were attached
four iron jougs, the terror of offenders. Many answered to the
call for recruits, the personal charm of the young Chevalier
possibly contributing to swell the number, one of whom was
the famous fiddler, Niel Gow, then a lad of eighteen. He had
played with others at the entertainment given to the Prince,
but his enthusiasm soon evaporated. He marched with the
army as far as Stirling, whence he returned to Dunkeld.
There is a curious story of another recruit whose name is
recorded on an old sundial in the town. The " Scots Magazine " of October, 1746, relates the incident, particulars being
copied from a York paper which gave a list of rebels tried at
York, five of whom were acquitted, amongst them John
Ballantine from Dunkeld. An extract is as follows:—" John
Ballantine acted as piper in Captain James Stewart's
Company in Lord George Murray's regiment. Several witnesses deponed ' that he was forced into the service by a
party of the rebels, who took him by violence out of his bed,
threatened to stab him if he did not go with them, and did
not allow him time even to put on his cloathes; and that
afterwards they placed a guard over him to prevent his
making his escape.' When the jury returned their verdict
' Not Guilty ' the poor fellow was in such a transport of joy
that he threw his bonnet up to the very roof of the Court and
cried out, ' My Lords and Gentlemen, I thank you. Not
Guilty! Not Guilty! Not Guilty! Pray God, bless King

DUNKELD IN THE 17TH CENTURY.

[*From an Old Print.*

THE ELL-MEASURE GAUGE.

[*Photo by H. Coates.*

George for ever. I'll serve him all the days of my life,' and immediately ran out into the Castleyard, with his irons on, took up a handful of channel water and drank his Majesty's health."

Clearly Ballantine had not been an ardent Jacobite. With regard to the irons mentioned, a descendant of his used to tell how she remembered, as a child, seeing the marks left by them, so roughly had he been used.

Prince Charles passed again through Dunkeld on his retreat to Culloden, but with vastly different feelings and with broken hopes. Lord George Murray afterwards despatched a party to Dunkeld, where they remained till the approach of the Hessians, the Duke of Cumberland's troops, from Perth. They then retired northward, and several skirmishes took place between them and the Hessians, but on the whole the latter showed no great wish to leave Dunkeld nor to meet the Athollmen. They treated the inhabitants very harshly, using the town as an advanced post, and, as the sympathies of the people were mostly Jacobite, they did not accord " Butcher " Cumberland's soldiers a very hearty welcome. It was probably to this occupation of the victors' troops that Culloden House, at present the Royal School, owed its name. One man at least in the Duke of Cumberland's army had an eye for other things than warfare. An English Volunteer Officer published a small book in 1747, conveying his impressions and observations as he marched through Perthshire. At first he " looked with dread upon the mountains, but dread soon passed into admiration." After a short stay in Perth, he was sent with two detachments, of 500 foot each, to Dunkeld. They left early on the 8th of February (1746), reaching Dunkeld at 4 o'clock. It was snowing hard when they started out but, he remarks, " they had a most agreeable variety " on the march, the hilly character of the country delighting him. The fir-clad peaks attracted his eye, and his comment thereon is that in a Roman Catholic country " no place would be more acceptable for the fixing of a crucifix to worship." He also describes the streams and waterfalls near Dunkeld and confesses that " with all these pleasing varieties we are able to endure great fatigue and hunger."

E

Others, as the country settled, found the scenery pleasing, and Dunkeld had its share of notable visitors, amongst whom might be mentioned Burns, Pennant, Dr. Garnett, Harriet Martineau, Wordsworth, and the poet Gray.

In 1809 the Bridge across the Tay was finished and this further facilitated travel, a new road being constructed northwards from the Bridge, joining Wade's road near Dowally.

A yearly Highland Gathering, claiming to be the first in Scotland, was inaugurated in 1822 for the express purpose of maintaining the garb, music and sports of the Highlands, and was continued until 1872. The Games now held annually in Birnam may be said to be a continuation of those formerly held in Dunkeld.

A visit which created great excitement was that of Queen Victoria and the Prince Consort in 1842. It was regarded as an event of supreme importance, being the first visit paid by a Hanoverian sovereign to a Jacobite stronghold and also the first visit of a reigning monarch since Queen Mary cf Scots.

A letter written by the shoemaker-poet, James Stewart, renders a graphic description in homely language of the excitement and preparations in Dunkeld. He writes thus to a friend—" The Queen! The Queen! Nothing but the Queen! . . . . I am to be sworn in as a rodman to clear the highway for the Queen's approach to the ' City of the Hills,' and I am to get half-a-crown for looking at Her Majesty and allowing my body to be squeezed and my toes crushed. All are rodmen here from the Bailie to the Bard. The Duchess of Atholl is making great preparations. She is going to give Her Majesty ' a chack o' meat ' on the green before the door. Correctly speaking there is a tent fitting up on the site of the old house of Dunkeld north of the Cathedral. Lord Glenlyon is to have in attendance 150 Highlanders and other Highland lairds are bringing tails of the bipeds. . . ."

A glorious monarchy man was proposing to have an arch stretched between Birnam and Newtyle—a distance of one mile. His project was laughed at.

" Ye're wrang," says he, " we could brawly streek a string across frae the tap o' the hills and hae broom cowes danglin' on it." " An amendment," said another, " what wad you think instead o' haein' broom cowes waffin' in the wind, to hae sklates on yer string, Tam?" (the said Tam being lessee of the slate quarry of Newtyle).

The enthusiasm was certainly great and a very full account is narrated in the " Memorial of the Royal Progress in Scotland," written by Sir Thomas Dick Lauder in 1847. There were triumphal arches all the way from Perth to Dunkeld. At Birnam Pass the Queen and Prince Albert had their first glimpse of Highland scenery, both showing marked appreciation. The Queen in a letter to her uncle, King Leopold, wrote:—" The situation of Dunkeld down in a valley surrounded by wooded hills, is very, very pretty."

Bonfires and flags everywhere testified to the loyalty of all. The morning was dull, but when the Royal party reached Dunkeld Bridge, the sun shone gloriously. A Gothic arch at the end of the bridge was a subject of general admiration; it was composed of heath and juniper (Murray badge) with a floral crown, and adorned besides with stuffed specimens of blackcock and eagle. Above were two deer with the words, " Welcome to Atholl." A battery was fired from Stanley Hill. A large body of Atholl Highlanders was in evidence after lunch, the pipers played and local Highlanders showed their agility and skill in reels and sword dances. In the Queen's words, " We lunched at Dunkeld, the beginning of the Highlands, in a tent—all the Highlanders in their fine dress being encamped there with their old swords and shields, looking very romantic, chiefly Lord Glenlyon's men."

At lunch Niel Gow's famous glass was in requisition, filled with Atholl brose. Thousands poured into the town to welcome their Queen. There is a story of a schoolboy, afterwards a prominent Magistrate in his native town, who ran all the way from Blairgowrie, playing truant for the day; there is another of a Dunkeld herd laddie who forgot his charge in the gratification of his curiosity, and there is still another of an old woman who pressed into the throng determined to speak to Her Majesty, " I ha'e a basketfu' o' bonnie aipples and I want her tae tak' them an' gie them tae her bairns."

Queen Victoria and various members of her family have

visited Dunkeld on several occasions; so have other Royalties, including the Empress Eugenie and her son.

The Disruption of the Church of Scotland also left its mark. The Rev. John Mackenzie, minister of the Cathedral, seceded in 1843. Through Lady Effingham's liberality a building was erected for worshippers, and on the same site, gifted by Fox Maule Ramsay, afterwards Earl of Dalhousie, another church, more commodious, was built in 1874, Dr. Duff, the great Indian missionary, opening it formally in the following year. The present minister of the congregation is the Rev. J. W. Hamilton, M.A., whose pastorate has extended over many years. The Perth to Dunkeld railway was opened in 1856, and in 1863 extended towards Inverness.

Dunkeld was again occupied by the military in 1868, a detachment of the Black Watch being stationed there during the disturbances known as the Toll Riots. It is on record, however, that the soldiers declared they had never resided in a more peaceful community. So pleasant was their visit that they left it with regret. Since then there have been several military occupations, mainly Volunteer Camps. The cavalry regiments of the Scottish Horse, first raised by the Marquis of Tullibardine (afterwards 8th Duke of Atholl) for service in the Boer War, encamped at Inver during the summers and were billeted in winter quarters in Dunkeld and Birnam from 1914-1917. They rendered valiant service in the Great War, and the Marquis received the appointment of Brigadier-General. Dunkeld still remains the headquarters of this regiment.

That Dunkeld and district did their duty nobly in the war is evinced by the record of losses graved on the Cairn Memorial at the Cross Roads, on the various Rolls of Honour, and in the Royal School Memorial.

By public subscription, a Fountain was erected at the Cross in 1866 to the memory of the 6th Duke of Atholl, who died in 1864. It was opened by his widow, Her Grace the Duchess Dowager, and is a handsome and beautiful piece of work.

After the railway opened many more illustrious visitors arrived, but the list is too long to be fully enumerated.

Several whose coming or sojourn in the district may be reckoned as events of importance may be mentioned.

Sir John Everett Millais, P.R.A., the well-known artist, was in residence for some time in Eastwood, St. Mary's Tower, and other houses. Many of his most famous pictures portray the beauty spots around. Of such are "The Sound of Many Waters," "Ower the hills an' far awa," "Winter Fuel," and others too numerous to mention.

In 1875 the Premier of Canada, the Hon. Alexander Mackenzie, visited Dunkeld, and was greeted with enthusiasm and honour. He was born in Logierait, but, the family removing to Dunkeld, many of his early years were spent there. That he and other members of his family did not forget the home of youth was shown for a long period by a yearly gift of apples to the town. Dunkeld also boasts connection with another Canadian statesman. This was the Hon. J. A. Stewart, Minister of Railways and Canals (in the Government of the Right Hon. Arthur Meighen) in the Canadian Parliament of 1921. He was born and died in Canada, but his father, Robert Stewart, was a native of Dunkeld, who emigrated in early life, revisiting his native town and relatives on several occasions.

Many statesmen have visited Dunkeld and Birnam. The Duke of Rutland, long Postmaster-General, when Lord John Manners, had a residence in Birnam, where he received many distinguished guests, such as Lord Salisbury. Butterstone House, in 1897, was the last place in Scotland honoured by a lengthy visit from the veteran statesman, the Right Hon. W. E. Gladstone.

Amongst later statesmen are Mr Lloyd George and Mr Baldwin, the latter of whom has been the guest on several occasions of the Duke and Duchess of Atholl at Eastwood House, Dunkeld. The Duchess of Atholl, who is often in residence at Eastwood, gained the distinction in 1924 of being the first woman in Scotland to become a Member of Parliament, she being returned then for West Perthshire and Kinross. Later on she gained another distinction on becoming the first woman in Britain to attain Cabinet rank.

The Restoration and Preservation of the Cathedral may also be regarded as historic and national events.

CHAPTER X.

Dunkeld Cathedral:
Restoration, Preservation, Existing Mounments.

THE Choir of the Cathedral was repaired in 1691 by the Atholl family to make it suitable as a place of worship for the Kirk of Scotland. State grants have been given at intervals for the same purpose, the most important being in 1815, when the building was fast hastening to ruin.

The restoration of the Choir to its former state as far as possible was accomplished in 1908 through the princely generosity of Sir Donald Currie of Garth. It was re-roofed with Caithness slabs, the end galleries and Atholl family seat removed and all restored, wherever possible, in keeping with the original design.

The seats are of oak, so are the carved pulpit screen and organ.

The stained glass in the East Window was also the gift of Sir Donald Currie, to whose memory a bronze tablet is affixed on the south wall. In addition, the tablet records the reopening of the Cathedral after the restoration in 1908, and the dedication of the East Window. In 1922, the Cathedral was handed over to the care of the nation by the Duke of Atholl, and the work of preservation was begun under the supervision of the Ancient and Historic Monuments Department of H.M. Office of Works. Not too soon was this ancient edifice handed over for preservation. Nearly a hundred years ago a local poet said of it—

> "Time, the destroyer, wi' his pick,
> Has gi'en the biggin' mony a prick."

And these lines are truer now than then. Within the last few decades decay has proceeded at a rapid rate, the stonework

of many of the beautiful windows in the roofless Nave having
fallen to the ground, where it lay in shapeless masses. In
every nook and cranny of the ruined walls plants had sprung
up, trees with spreading roots and clusters of wallflowers.
Two of the greatest enemies after the clashing destruction
of war were clinging ivy and birds. To quote again the poet
James Stewart, already referred to—

" Green ivy cleeds the roofless wa's,
    Soughs through each arch the wind that blaws,
While here and there in dusky raws,
        The feathered nations
    O' hoolets, kaes and huddy craws
        Haud consultation."

Preservation, not restoration, is the keynote. Crumbling
mouldings and carvings, also the stone framework of windows,
are carefully treated and rendered watertight to prevent
further decay Huge growths of ivy, the products of centuries,
were removed from the walls. These long clinging trails of
lustrous green had lent a picturesque appearance to the ruin,
and their removal makes it look shorn and bare, so that a
little natural regret may be felt at this necessary destruction.
Specially is this the case in the small lateral porch at the
south wall, formerly a beautiful sight, summer or winter.
In the time of roses, sprays twined through the ivy and
clambered over the porch, their white and pink flowers peeping
out from amongst the glossy leaves. The porch is bare now,
devoid of twining sprays, but the doorway to which it leads
is seen to advantage and other remains of former ornamentation. The side walls of the porch, however, show little
ornamentation, and are so out of keeping with the rest of it
as to raise a suspicion that they are a later addition.

In the basement room of the Tower or Belfry remains
of early paintings are yet seen on the wall, the subjects of
which are rather difficult to determine. One figure is suggested
as being a portrayal of Solomon acting as arbiter between the
two women who claimed the same child. If this were so, the
subject was probably chosen as befitting a Court of Justice.
In this room or consistory of the early church have been held
various Dunkeld Courts of Justice. It is in good preservation
yet.

The ground extending from the entrance gate to the

boundary fence beyond the building and sloping towards the Tay now provides an open space with seats for visitors. Previous to 1560 this part was the place of interment, but since then, until lately, was occupied by "The Cottage" and gardens. The view is one of quiet, yet striking, beauty. The noble river sweeping on in silent majesty, the picturesque arches of the stately bridge which spans its flow, the meeting of the Braan and Tay, with the classic brow of Birnam Hill just beyond, the historic ruin almost under the shadow of craggy peaks—all combine to form a scene seldom equalled.

The lawn is softly green, and there still rises to a noble height near the Tower one of the parent larches brought to Scotland in a carpet bag by Menzies of Culdares when young plants, and planted in 1738. It is rather strange to learn that these trees were at first treated as hothouse plants, pining and fading under such treatment, until finally they were put outside to live or die as they pleased. One fell in 1909, and from its timber various articles have been made as mementos and curiosities.

Although the ancient glories of Dunkeld Cathedral, such as its altars and paintings, have disappeared, there are still many interesting relics of the past. Several monuments and tombs have survived the destroyers' hands.

Entering by the east door to the right, behind the Screen, are seen the two early Christian monumental slabs described in Chapter II. Between them, on the east wall, is a monument which has given rise to controversy, that to the Black Watch. It is certainly a gruesome and realistic piece of work. Over it hung formerly the tattered regimental colours which are now above the Atholl family pew. The monument is executed in white marble by Sir John Steele, R.S.A., and was unveiled by the Duchess Dowager of Atholl in 1872. The battlefield, with its slaughter and carnage, destruction and horrors, is represented; the centre figure, an officer of the regiment, stands with bared head surveying the terrible results of deadly strife. This monument was erected by officers of the corps, and bears a suitable inscription with the names of the many battlefields in which the regiment won fame.

"And heroes haunt those old Cathedral walls."

Opposite is the stone sarcophagus of the Wolf of Badenoch, thus named from his ferocity. Alister More Mac an Righ, third son of Robert II., died in 1394. He was cruel and merciless as a wolf, sparing none; his fury fell upon all, Church, noble, and burgher, but his epitaph reads, "Bona Memoriæ," and that he died in the odour of sanctity at peace with the Church is indicated by the clasped hands on the breast of the statue. A graphic description of the Wolf's penance, prescribed by the Church, can be read in Sir Thomas Dick Lauder's novel, "The Wolf of Badenoch." Into the Blackfriars Monastery, in Perth, the penitent walked barefooted and clad in penitential robes through gaping, wondering crowds, and there confessed his sins publicly before the Bishops of Dunkeld, Dunblane and St. Andrews. The humiliation and subjugation of such a fierce and influential personage vividly portrays the power of the Church of Rome in the 14th century. The sarcophagus is still in tolerable preservation and the Latin inscription easily deciphered. The statue is in armour with a lion at the feet, a lamb in its clutches. A groat of Robert II., found in this coffin, was presented to the Perth Museum.

Near this statue on the east wall is a bronze in memory of the Cameronian officers who fell in the Great War. It was erected by relatives, and is placed beside that commemorating Lieut.-Colonel Cleland of the same regiment, who fell in the Battle of Dunkeld. A slab to the memory of Rev. John Robb recalls the stirring tale of Grace Darling, and the wreck of the Forfarshire, for after a short incumbency Mr. Robb was drowned in that shipwreck, 1838, and was buried in Bamborough Churchyard.

Another tablet is to the memory of Major-General Sir Robert Dick of Tullymet, who fell at Sabron in 1846.

Near the pulpit is the Hagioscope, a small opening in the wall, placed in an oblique direction to enable the worshippers, in parts where the altars were not visible, to see the Elevation of the Host. Such openings were sometimes termed Leper windows, or "Squints."

The mutilated statue of Bishop Sinclair, the honoured friend of Robert the Bruce, lies in the North Aisle, while the statue of another Bishop is also preserved. This is the founder of the Nave, Bishop Cardney, whose tomb is in a recess of the south wall of the ruins, dated 1420. There is a Latin inscription on the top, but much of the lettering is defaced. The statue is full length with mitre, robe and staff. The Bishop himself was buried in St. Ninian's Chapel (Atholl Street), and the monument originally erected there, but afterwards brought to the Cathedral. Opposite, in the north wall, is the Cardney family monument with a vault below. Still within the ruins and near the stone marking the grave of Lieut.-Colonel Cleland lies General Charles Edward Stewart, Count Rochenstart, son of the Duchess of Albany, daughter of Prince Charlie, who was born in Rome and died in Dunkeld, 1854, from the result of an accident. Returning from Inverness, after a visit to Lord Lovat, the coach in which he was travelling was upset near Inver. He was conveyed to the Atholl Arms Hotel, Dunkeld, where he died. Those who met him testified to the charm of manner which made it apparent that he was a true descendant of the Prince who had won so many Highland hearts. An anecdote lingers in Inver to the effect that he sent a sum of money to several women in Inver who had rushed to help the injured. This they invested in Stewart tartan ribbon and wore it for many a day. Perhaps no more fitting place for the " Last of the Stewarts," as he styled himself, could be found than within the walls of Dunkeld Cathedral, close to the land of Atholl, from whose glens and valleys had poured many gallant men to fight and die for his grandsire.

Mention is sometimes made of an epitaph written by Pennycook on Marjory Scott, said to be buried here in 1728, but it is not to be found on stone. MacLean's Guide gives it in full. Part of it runs—

" Betwixt my cradle and my grave were seen,
Seven mighty Kings of Scotland and a Queen.
I saw the Stewart race thrust out, nay more,
I saw our country sold for English ore.
Our numerous nobles, who have famous been
Sunk to the lowly number of sixteen,
I have an end of all perfection seen."

Bishop Brown's memorial window, already referred to, is in the north wall near the Tower, and there are besides other monuments of interest, both modern and ancient, amongst them a rough unhewn Ionic Cross to Dr. Murray, a true surgeon of the old school. The Rev. T. Wilson, a faithful pastor, who died in 1877, is buried here, as his tombstone records. His successor, the Rev. T. R. Rutherford, M.A., died shortly before the attainment of his jubilee as minister. He is buried in Dowally Churchyard.

The great bell is protected within a wooden erection which sadly muffles its tone. Formerly this bell rang at six o'clock in the morning and tolled the curfew at eight each evening. The former practice was discontinued many years ago, the latter only during the war, and has, as yet, not been resumed.

The Cathedral grounds are entered from Cathedral Street, a narrow, quaint street fully bearing out the ancient character of the little city. The view through the gate along the street is very picturesque, and is greatly improved since the plates of iron across the bars have been removed. The gate itself is a beautiful piece of workmanship and once stood at the entrance to the original Dunkeld House, the avenue to which can still be traced behind the building in present use as an Armoury, near the Fountain.

CHAPTER XI.

Schools and Education.

DUNKELD being one of the earliest civic and ecclesiastical foundations in Scotland, it is but natural to assume that it had also educational facilities at a very early period. It is probable that even in prehistoric times, judging from the stone monuments in the district that the Druid priests expounded and taught their doctrines in Dunkeld; it being a capital of Mid Pictavia or Caledonia, would be a natural centre of such learning.

Church schools were founded in Atholl and Strathtay by early missionaries, but the educational history of Scotland is generally imputed to have had its beginnings in the days of St. Columba, who first founded schools in Iona and elsewhere.

The " Muintir Kailli-an-Find " or Collegiate Church, founded by the Dalriadic Scots near Dunkeld about 600, would send apostles or teachers all around. The establishment afterwards of a monastery, and a church foundation about 800 would certainly make the beginnings of a school in Dunkeld, for neophytes at least, as the church was then the great agent of progress and civilisation, also the repository of learning. The celebration of church services required a certain degree of education only to be found within the walls of such establishments. Music would be taught; the Columban monks chanted their Psalms in a peculiar manner, generally in the open air; this service of praise was even sometimes called the " Dunkeld Litany." A knowledge of Latin was essential, and the monks, in addition to copying the Scriptures and other books, gave training in art. They also gave secular instruction and taught many useful things.

Many of the Abbots of Dunkeld were noted men of learning, such as St. Adamnan, the biographer of Columba; "Edelrade," Abbot of Dunkeld and Earl of Fife, a son of Malcolm III., encouraged education to such a degree that in a document dated 1100, he gave grants for the maintenance of learning to the Culdees in Lochleven, where there was a famous library.

In 1127, although the Culdees lost their power, on the changing of their Monastery into a Cathedral Church, the Bishops appointed to the See of Dunkeld were mostly notable scholars, who, by their example, gave an impetus to learning. There were amongst others Thomas Lawder, who wrote the life of a predecessor, and the famous Gavin Douglas.

Canon Myln, writing in 1515, gives an account of a school founded by the Chancellor of Dunkeld Cathedral, which may be regarded as the precursor of the Royal School. He says—"Mr George Brown, a near relative of the Bishop's . . . in honour of our Lady of Consolation, erected in the Church of St. George, a scholastic chaplain and head-master of a grammar school. The church may expect many good grammatical scholars from this establishment if kept up."

Of the Prebendary of Muckersie, another member of the Chapter of Dunkeld, Myln tells that at his own charge, he educated some good men. So did another, Mr. Alexander Richardson, who "educated promising young men at his own expense, some for monks, some for priests, and others for the service of the quire as he found they had a turn." Various officials are also commended for their skill in grammar.

The school established by Chancellor Brown in the Cathedral Chapel of St. George may probably have been carried on until the Reformation, when the Chapel fell in the destruction of the Cathedral. Seven years afterwards, in 1567, King James VI. made a Grant for the erection of a Grammar School at Dunkeld, and it was endowed under a Royal Warrant of that date.

In the Charter granted then, the King gave the Earl of Atholl and his successors the patronage of the school.

Changes, of course, keeping pace with the varying educational requirements of the nation, have taken place in the administration of grants and endowments.

Under the Educational Endowments (Scotland) Act 1882, a scheme was drawn up for the administration of the endowments known as the Royal School of Dunkeld, hitherto held and administered under a Royal Warrant, dated 2nd February 1567, and the Bishopric Rents of Dunkeld, hitherto held and administered under a grant by King William III., dated 29th February, 1696. This scheme was approved by the Queen in Council, 15th October, 1889. A governing body was then constituted called the Governors, consisting of five persons, one of whom was His Grace, the Duke of Atholl, another appointed by him, and the remaining three by the School Boards of Caputh, Little Dunkeld, and Dunkeld and Dowally district. During the many educational changes which have occurred, this endowment has been retained. At one period, however, its withdrawal was threatened by the Commissioners of Woods and Forests, who administer the Crown revenues. In conjunction with the Perthshire Authority and the Dunkeld Parish Council, the Governors sought legal advice. On the intimation that there was a legal claim to this grant in perpetuity, the Commissioners agreed to continue the payment.

This 1696 grant by William III. was made with the consent of the Lord Commissioners of his Treasury and Exchequer. The extract from the report throws a light on the times:—"Considering how useful and necessary schools of learning are for instructing all youth in the knowledge and practice of a religion, and for introducing civilitie and policie and order, and that the rents belonging to the late Bishops in our ancient Kingdome of Scotland, and now fallen into our hands, are most propper to be applyed for the ends and uses aforesaid . . . and that throw the neglect and iniquity of times past schools have not been erected as they ought to have been in the bounds of the Highlands of Perthshire . . . . nor sufficient fees and allowances appointed for the masters and teachers in the few schools that have been erected."

In Hunter's " Diocese of Dunkeld " there are several allusions to the schools in the Presbytery, amongst them Dunkeld and Little Dunkeld. Acts of Parliament passed in 1633 and 1641 regarding schools and maintenances for schoolmasters were not obeyed in this Presbytery, any more than in any other parts of Scotland, but after the Act of 1696 some efforts were made. The Presbytery reports in 1707 that there are schools at Dunkeld, Douly, Caputh, and other centres. In 1716, it was reported that in Little Dunkeld, Caputh and other parishes, there was no salary for a schoolmaster according to law.

Notwithstanding the Endowment Grant of 1696, educational matters in Dunkeld could not have been altogether satisfactory, for in a Memorial of 1716 to the Society for Propagating Christian Knowledge, the Dunkeld Presbytery, stating their opinion as to the educational requirements in the Highlands of Atholl, make the following suggestion with regard to Dunkeld :—" The toun of Dunkeld, situate at the foot of the Highlands, where there is good accommodation for schollars, would be a most proper place for gentlemen and others in the Highlands, for ane nigh to send their children to be educated and well instructed in Latine, Greek, Arithmetick, which for the present has no legal sallary, in regaird there are little arable lands circumjacent. So that there being nothing but houses and gardens in the said toun no competency hitherto could be obtained for a schoolmaster from the inhabitants; wherefore it is our humble opinion that were there a fixed schoolmaster with due encouragement there, if it were but to the value of twintie pound sterling, and five pound sterling for an under teacher, it would tend much not only to the advantage of the said Highlands, but also to that of many parts of the low country near adjacent."

It appears as if such a salary ought to have been forthcoming. In the deed of the foundation of the Royal School, 1567, reference is made to various prebends, and the sums payable yearly from them for the support of the schoolmaster is quoted in Hunter's " Diocese." The chaplainry of Invar was charged with payment of £10, others with £4, and so on. Before the Reformation it was stated that some of this

money, with £4 of the rental of the hospituim of the Bishop
of Dunkeld in Perth had been applied to the support of certain boys called " blew freiris," who served in the Cathedral
choir.

In the Statistical Account of Dunkeld, 1798, the
Grammar School is mentioned with the salary of the schoolmaster as £34 sterling, dues payable to the Chaplain of St.
Ninian's, and an official dwelling-house. These dues were
20 merks Scots, 2 bolls of coal and 2 dozen of poultry. From
the circumstance of the Rector of the Royal School thus receiving dues payable to a chaplain, he also received the title
of Chaplain of St. Ninian's. This chapel, built in 1420, had
been endowed out of the rents of Mucklari.

At the burning of Dunkeld in 1689, the school building
was, of course, destroyed, but the scholars were accommo
dated for some time in another attached to the east gable of
the Cathedral, which still shows the marks. For a considerable period afterwards the Royal School was held in a
building facing the Tay, in Cathedral Street, but in 1891
another change took place, and this building ceased to be the
Royal School, becoming in later days the headquarters of
the Scottish Horse regiment.

Culloden House, opposite the Fountain, where the Market
Cross once stood, was converted into school buildings, and
became the Dunkeld Royal School. It was an old, roomy
house, once an inn, but a private house when brought into
school use.

The Dunkeld Royal School has therefore had a long and
honourable history; and as an educational centre, it may be
seen that Dunkeld occupied a place of importance in the
county. Until railway facilities opened up the country, giving
easy access to larger towns in the south, this school gave
good education to the sons of many of the ancient Highland
families, and scholars travelled long distances.

In a list of the Schoolmasters of Dunkeld, 1659-1686,
given by Hunter, one is " Mr. Andrew Malloch," who had
been a " Doctor of the Grammar School of Perth," whilst
another, Mr. James Ross, was, on leaving Dunkeld, appointed
Master of the Grammar School at Perth. He was succeeded

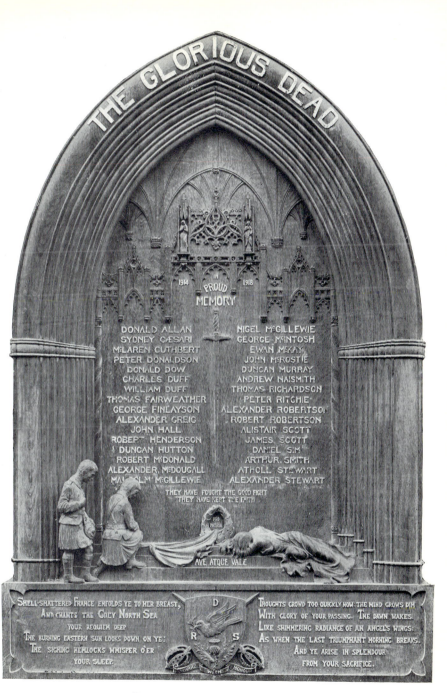

ROYAL SCHOOL WAR MEMORIAL.

by Alexander Robertson, who afterwards entered the ministry. Robertson was designated preacher at Little Dunkeld in 1684, but still retained his office of schoolmaster at Dunkeld; then was fully admitted minister of Little Dunkeld two years after. These masters figured largely in the law deeds of that period as witnesses. One, Andrew Creichtoun, is designated as Schoolmaster of the Grammar School in Dunkeld, 1648.

Jerome Stone, schoolmaster in Dunkeld in the next century, contributed his quota to the Ossianic translations. He is mentioned in Brown's history of the Highlands as a native of Fife, who had acquired a "knowledge of the Gaelic language during some years' residence in Dunkeld, where he kept a school. He was the third person who collected several of the ancient poems of the Highlands, and the first who called attention to their beauty in a letter from Dunkeld addressed to the 'Author of the Scots Magazine.' This letter is quoted in full in the 'History' as displaying considerable talent." In 1752, Stone contributed to the Scots Magazine an English version of Bishop Douglas' Prologue to the Twelfth Book of the Æneid, "A Morning in May." In 1756, his rhyming translation of a Gaelic poem appeared in another number of the Scots Magazine.

Another literary Rector was Dr. MacCulloch, who flourished in the beginning of the 19th century and whose "Course of Reading" was long popular in schools throughout Scotland. He published "The Highland and Western Isles" with "Guides to Perthshire and Dunkeld." These were elaborate works, and contain very fine descriptive writing. He entered the ministry, and went to Greenock.

The Statistical Account of Dunkeld tells that a Sunday School was founded in 1789 by Jane, Duchess of Atholl. There were fees for this, paid partly by the Duchess and partly by parents. One of the rules was that the pupils had to walk in regular order on Sunday with the master to church, where they were allotted seats. A public examination was also held of this Sunday School. This same Duchess founded a "Female School," where sewing and tambouring

F

(a species of embroidery) were chiefly taught. However, a
lesson in English was read daily. The mistress here also
was paid partly by the Duchess and partly by parents.

Although originally the Royal School numbered amongst
its pupils girls as well as boys, the custom had fallen into
disuse, probably because of the establishment of such Female
Schools and also for want of space. A Girls' Industrial School was
erected by the Duchess of Atholl at her own expense in 1853.
A plain but good education was given there, although at first
a very large portion of time was devoted to industrial work,
the pupils being supplied with yellow calico aprons trimmed
with red braid for that purpose. Another feature, too, of
the school was that for a number of years it was regarded as
almost a church school, and pupils of Free Church parentage,
though not refused admittance, were debarred from certain
privileges, such as becoming pupil teachers. A more en-
lightened policy, however, soon prevailed, and the school was
largely attended and appreciated. The last teacher was
Miss Illingworth, a lady of powerful personality, long remembered as an excellent teacher. In 1898, on the death of
the Duchess Dowager of Atholl, in whom Dunkeld lost a
friend, the Girls' Industrial School was merged into the Royal
School, where the old scholastic reputation is fully maintained. The present Rector is Mr Henry Crombie, M.A.

In 1910, an interesting event, forming a link in the Empire
chain, occurred in the school history. This was an exchange
of flags with the Dunkeld State School, Victoria, Australia.
Across the sea the Dunkeld Royal School sent the Union
Jack " in a casket designed by a Dunkeld boy (William
Campbell Borrie), and made by an old Dunkeld boy (Hugh
Robertson) from an old Dunkeld tree." This old Dunkeld
tree was one of the parent larches which was cut down in
1908, and the wood for the casket was gifted by the Duke of
Atholl. In return the school children of Dunkeld, in
Australia, sent the Australian flag in a polished blackwood
case.

The Higher Grade department was instituted in 1907 and
has justified its existence. That the pupils, too, have nobly

fulfilled the school motto, "Forward with Honour," given
by the present Rector, is evinced by the School Memorial,
unveiled in 1922 by the Lady Helen Tod, for those who fell
in the Great War.   This artistic and beautiful memorial
was designed by William Campbell Borrie, L.R.C.P., and
S.E., a former pupil of the school, who also composed the
verse graven on it beginning,

"Shell-shattered France enfolds thee to her breast."

There are thirty-two names upon the Memorial.   The
memorial was erected by public subscription, mainly
through the efforts of the present Rector, supported by the
various members of the staff, former pupils, and a standing
committee of three, viz., Misses E. Stewart, J. Bruce and
F. Macdonald.

The Perthshire Education Authority have it in view to
close this school and erect a combined school for Dunkeld and
Birnam, near the Cross Roads, Little Dunkeld, not far from
which there was, in former days, the Parochial School.   This
latter was closed on the passing of the Scotch Education Act
in 1872, and the pupils transferred to Torwood, Birnam, where
the Free Church School was held.   Both schools were thus
united.

Other schools there were in Dunkeld. ladies' schools,
Gaelic schools, Dame schools—those latter principally for in-
fants.   The memory of one of these is still green.   It was
in, or near, the Cross Wynd, and the teacher, Isabella
Robertson, is best remembered by the soubriquet given her by
irreverent pupils, Tibby Toddles.   She taught all her pupils in
one room out of one Book, the Bible.   Occasionally, the
Shorter Catechism might be used.   She required to fear no
Inspector and studied her own ideas of pronunciation.   For
long, her pupils were recognised by words such as se-pul-chre
or Cap-er-naum, and when a very hard word appeared her
comment was, "That's Latin, dawtie, pass on."   A beautiful
and touching description of this old lady and her pupils is
found in James Stewart's sketch, "Eppie Broon," and as
an example of ordinary education in the early days of the
19th century the poem is worthy of quotation.

"Imagine a woman, o' threescore and ten,
Leanin' owre a bit staff wi' a pike at the en'!

.   .   .   .

Gie a sow-backit mutch and an auld-fashioned goon,
An' there's something before you like wee Eppie Broon.

.   .   .   .

She fends frae the swirls o' poverty's shock
By skuilin' the bairns o' hard-workin' fock.

.   .   .   .

For weekly, uncawkit, as Monday comes roon'
There's tippence sent wi' them for auld Eppie Broon.

.   .   .   .

When time's at your wairin', oh, spend a half-oor
To see a' her scholars ranged roon on her floor,
Her kingies and queenies, her tots and her cocks,
A' bizzin' an' bummin' like bees in a box.
Wee Curly Mary is puzzled at D,
An' gleg little Janet is scratchin' at E,
But Charlie's a hero, an' braks a' the toon
He's forrit at izzit, wi' auld Eppie Broon.

.   .   .   .

There' a class for the Bible, the Carritch, the Psalms,
Whase dux is preferred to a seat near the jambs.
Verse aboot's read aloud—some hae to spell
Faster than Eppie can weel dae hersel'.

.   .   .   .

And, oh, how delighted the wee totums stand
When she tells o' the joys o' a heavenly land.

.   .   .   .

It's no wrang to say that our Maker looks doon
Wi' a smile o' approval on auld Eppie Broon."

Such schools are things of the past, but they, too, had an honourable place.

CHAPTER XII.

The Mackintosh Library.

ANOTHER Gaelic scholar in addition to Jerome Stone, Master of the Royal School, who had a connection with Dunkeld, was the Revd. Donald Mackintosh. In the buildings occupied by the Royal School, both former and present, was a room devoted to a collection of books named the Mackintosh Library. Through carelessness and neglect in bygone years, the ponderous old volumes gradually have become, many of them, torn and dilapidated, whilst others have been lost. On the transference of the school from the old building near the Cathedral to Culloden House, the books were also removed thither.

In this library are still many interesting and valuable volumes, if not to the general reader, certainly so to the student and scholar.

The collection was gifted to the Cathedral City of Dunkeld by the Revd. Donald Mackintosh, Episcopal Minister of Strathtay, who claimed to be the last non-juring priest in Scotland. He was one of that body of ecclesiastics who refused to acknowledge the Kingship of the House of Hanover, protesting against the Foreign Succession and the Whiggish principles of a British Hierarchy. It will therefore be easily granted that from the firm but solitary nature of his stand, this minister was no ordinary person, but a man of strong will and opinions, even to obstinacy, an account of his life and work confirming this view.

The following particulars concerning this non-juring priest are quoted, by permission, from an interesting and scholarly pamphlet written by the Revd. W. M. Tuke, formerly incumbent of St. Mary's Episcopal Church, Birnam. In this pamphlet indebtedness is acknowledged to an article which appeared in Stephen's Episcopal Magazine for July, 1836. and to a biography, compiled by one Alexander Campbell, who had personal knowledge of Mackintosh and various members of the family to which he belonged.

Donald Mackintosh was born in 1743, near Killiecrankie, his father being a small farmer on the Urrard Estate. He must have received a fairly good education at the nearest village school, for he went to Edinburgh and there felt qualified to seek success as a teacher. His efforts in this line were not satisfactory, or he may have desired a change, but, whatever the reason, at the age of 31, he was employed as a postman. A private individual, Williamson by name, had proved himself a pioneer of the penny post and established an institution of that kind in Edinburgh. He employed a number of men to collect and deliver letters and of these Donald Mackintosh was one, wearing a uniform cap on which was printed in gilt letters " Williamson's Penny Post."

However, his ambition was scotched, not killed! It had only lain dormant; and he endeavoured to woo fame in the guise of literature, after he had been successful in receiving several good appointments in another line. Becoming tutor in the family of Sir George Stewart of Grandtully, he was well remunerated. He made a tour through Lochaber, and began to gather material for a work which he afterwards published, " Gaelic Proverbs," a copy of which may be found in the Library of the Perth Literary and Antiquarian Museum. As he was considered a good Gaelic scholar, the work is of recognised value. Interested as he was in the Legends and Melodies of the Highlands, he collected many of them. He was fortunate in having various friends who were able and willing to assist him, amongst them Henry Mackenzie, author of " Man of Feeling," and after the publication, in 1785, of his Proverbs, he was offered a situation as clerk in the office of an Edinburgh lawyer, which appointment he held for several years.

Still he was not content. His ambition lay in another direction. He sought ordination and received it, being afterwards regarded by various Jacobite families as the only true

Pastor or Priest left in Scotland. He has some claim to that distinction when the reasons offered from a Jacobite standpoint are studied.

On the death of Prince Charles Edward Stewart, the Protestant Jacobites found themselves in a curious predicament. The successor to the throne, from their point of view, was his brother Henry, a Cardinal of the Church of Rome. Thereupon many Jacobites at last transferred their allegiance to the reigning house and joined in the prayers for King George. Notwithstanding their prejudice against a Hanoverian king, they preferred him to the Pope of Rome. A few still remained staunch to the House of Stewart. Of these, Bishop Rose of Dunblane and James Brown, Presbyter at Montrose, were the only two clergymen who refused to acknowledge the Headship of Hanover over the Scottish Episcopal Church. Bishop Rose had consecrated Brown to the Episcopate and Brown had ordained Donald Mackintosh to the Deaconate and Priesthood, he being the only non-juring priest ordained as such in Scotland. The validity of their ordination has been questioned, but Mackintosh himself had no doubt on the subject and alluded to himself as " The Revd. Donald Mackintosh, a Priest of the Old Scots Episcopal Church, and last of the non-jurant clergy in Scotland."

He was highly esteemed by these valiant old Jacobites, who never swerved from their belief that he was the only true Priest left in Scotland.

He had a wide pastoral district, stretching from Edinburgh to Loch Katrine, thence to lone Glentilt, on to bonnie Glenshee, and north-east to Banff, a range altogether of more than a hundred miles. Still he found time to gather the large collection of books he afterwards bequeathed to the "Cathedral City of Dunkeld."

His latter days were spent in comparative comfort, several legacies falling his way and, in addition, he had received a good appointment as Translator of the Gaelic language and Keeper of the Gaelic Records to the Royal Highland Society of Scotland. In 1808, his health failed and he was unable to undertake his yearly journey throughout his pastorate.

Shortly after, he died and was buried in Greyfriars, Edinburgh, but no stone records his death or marks his grave.

In this collection or library there are many curious and interesting volumes; some of them are rare, but unfortunately several valuable works are now amissing, lost or destroyed. There are numerous theological works, as might be expected, and old histories, such as Holinshed's Scottish Chronicle. Translations of Ossian abound, and copies of the Poems of Gavin Douglas, and Blind Harry's Wallace. A copy of Allan Ramsay's Poems is thus proudly annotated on the fly-leaf, " Given to me by the poet's own hand."

Jacobite pamphlets, too, are numerous and interesting, as well as treatises Presbyterial and Episcopal; Calvin, of course, is represented and John Knox.

The catalogue drawn up in 1823 by Dr M'Culloch, Rector of the Royal School, who acted as Librarian, is still in existence.

In his will Mackintosh appointed Curators to administer the affairs, two of whom were to be in perpetuity, the Minister of Dunkeld and the nearest Episcopal Minister to the City of Dunkeld.

The readers of a former age boldly attacked bulky volumes, heavy both in matter and weight. The Mackintosh Library is not the only example of a solid collection in the district. The Minutes of a Reading Society formed in Inshewan (Birnam) have been preserved and are of interest to the curious. The title page is beautifully transcribed by hand, and would adorn any age.

The Inshewan Reading Society was proposed in 1796 by some persons in the three Inshewans, Easter, Wester and Middle. The Rules and Regulations are carefully drawn up and very rigid, *if enforced*. One reads rather strangely, " If any member resides twenty miles from the seat of the society he shall no more be considered a member; but . . . he shall have it in his power to transfer his share of the Library to his son, or his brother or his son-in-law providing he is of good moral character."

The books purchased and read eagerly, as the Minutes reveal, are no light reading. One Minute records how the members met and balloted for the privilege of reading, in rotation, Dean Prideaux' "Connections." Another records a proposal to remove the books from the house of Mr Wm. Harris, where they had at first been housed, as a larger room was required. " The members will meet and carry the Books to William Stewart's in Western Inshewan. Mr William M'Ara was appointed Chaplain to walk in Front of the Procession carrying Dr. Doddridge's Family Expositor, and to consecrate the books after being placed in the New Library with a Prayer." When the removal did take place, it is related that, " The Meeting adjourned to Birnam Inn . . . and after partaking of a plentiful dinner resumed the business of the Society . . ." Business concluded, " then the country beverage, Whisky Toddy, was ordered and the members continued together till a late hour. Many appropriate toasts were drunk in course of the evening and the members inspired by the enlivening spirit of genuine Glenlivat sung many national airs with real Scotch glee."

This Society was wound up in 1854, but it is interesting to know that a bookcase containing the books is still in the possession of a descendant of one of the founders. In the Reading Room of the Birnam Institute is a good modern Library and the same is also found in the Dunkeld Reading Room, where the Rural Libraries' Committee, under the administration of the Perthshire Education Authority, keep up a good supply of books in connection with the Carnegie Trust.

CHAPTER XIII.

Dunkeld Bridge.

THERE is an old print of Dunkeld, dated 1693, in which the general aspect is so unfamiliar as to be almost unrecognisable at the first glance. Closer inspection reveals that it is mainly the absence of the Bridge which causes the unfamiliarity. The most noticeable feature is the bold, unbroken sweep of the river, with the steep declivities dipping into the water, clear, and free from the heaps of stones which now deflect the currents. The rocky contour of Craig-y-barns, bare, jagged and treeless, in the background, shows little change, but there are several houses west of the Cathedral and a large square building is very conspicuous. This latter was Dunkeld House, which played so prominent a part in the Cameronian defences in 1689, and was pulled down in 1829. Severel boats on the river complete a picture which drew admiration even in a period when Nature's beauties were seldom prized.

Gray, the poet, in a letter to Walpole (Earl of Orford) gives a fine description of his advance to Dunkeld in the days before the Bridge was built. " The road came to the brow of a steep descent, and the sun then setting between two woods of oak, we saw far below us the river Tay come sweeping along at the bottom of a precipice at least 150 feet deep, clear as glass, full to the brim, and very rapid in its course. Down by the side of the river, under the thickest shades is seated the town of Dunkeld; in the midst of it stands a ruined Cathedral—the tower and shell of the building still entire, a little beyond it a large house belonging to the Duke of Atholl."

A bridge had long been felt to be a necessity. The river was often swollen, delay and danger were both incurred in the attempt to cross either by the fords or the ferries. Many noted men and travellers have crossed it near Dunkeld. Bruce and his army, after the defeat of Methven, 1306, had crossed at the " King's Ford " and passed northwards, Montrose crossed and re-crossed, Burns used the Inver Ferry, near the Cathedral. Pennant, in his " Travels," gives an amusing account of his trip across the Tay, the boat being attended by a tame swan, which was perpetually soliciting the favours of the passengers.

The present Bridge is not the first which spanned the Tay at Dunkeld. So long ago as 1461, Bishop Lawder laid the foundations of a bridge to be constructed partly of stone and partly of timber. This one was carried on by his successor, Bishop Livingtoun, but it is unknown if this bridge ever attained completion. Again, Bishop Brown began a stone bridge near his Palace and saw an arch of it finished in 1513. During his summer residence at Dunkeld, in the last year of his life, it was his amusement and recreation to watch from his chamber window the building of the Bridge. In his will he wrote, " All the share of St. Colme's patrimony which falls to me, I bequeath for the support of the Church and Bridge of Dunkeld and maintenance of the poor."

His executors drove the piles for other two arches. Bishop Douglas continued the work, and as Myln says, " Upon receiving two hundred and forty pound from Bishop George's executors, the work was brought the length that all foot passengers had an easy passage." This bridge was probably swept away. Shortly before the present one was built, when the river was exceptionally low, part of an arch on the north bank became visible, as were also piles supporting the second and third arches. These have been seen again in recent years.

When the military road from Fort George to Dunkeld was in course of construction, General Wade came to the latter place with the intention of building a bridge across the Tay. It is related that he desired an interview or consultation with the Duke of Atholl on the subject, but his request was so coolly and carelessly received that his dissatisfaction was great and he retired in anger to Aberfeldy, where he built his bridge instead of at Dunkeld.

The present Bridge, which forms such a pleasing feature
in the landscape, is mainly due to the efforts of John, 4th
Duke of Atholl. In 1803 an Act was obtained to build a Bridge
and to make roads and approaches thereto. It was designed
by Telford and opened in 1809, as the date on the middle
arch denotes. A medal was struck to commemorate the building, one being preserved in the Perth Antiquarian Museum.

There are seven arches, five beneath which the river flows
and two on land. The entire length is 685 feet and the width
26½ feet. The height of the centre is 90 feet. During its
construction the current of the river was diverted, as may be
gathered from the study of old prints.

The cost naturally was great and the Grant paid by the
Commissioners of High Roads and Bridges was not sufficient
to defray expenses. Money was borrowed on the security of
the Tolls, the Ferries were abolished and the right of portage
solely given to the Bridge. No pedestrian or vehicle was
allowed to pass without paying portage dues, which were
collected on behalf of the Duke of Atholl, who had incurred
the chief expense and lost the ferry dues. As time passed, the
toll levied on each foot passenger caused a great deal of
friction, leading to a series of regrettable disturbances known
as the Toll Riots, the memory of which still lingers. Whilst
acknowledging on the one hand that the Atholl family had
been responsible for the great part of the expenses, on the
other it was asserted that the pontage dues paid for years had
amply covered the debt. The grievance was felt more keenly
after the opening of the Dunkeld and Perth railway in 1856.
Either through stupidity or the prejudiced objections shown
by many landowners when railways were first constructed,
the Railway Station was placed at some distance from Dunkeld and, worse still, on the opposite side of the river. The
blunder was soon recognised, but the deed was done, and
each citizen was forced to pay toll ere he could enter upon a
railway journey; no visitor could enter Dunkeld by rail without paying his " bawbee." The citizens grumbled that the
custom even exposed them to ridicule. It was a common joke
in the countryside that Dunkeld folks were closed within gates
when " curfew rang," for the gatekeeper retired then from

his sentry box and had to be rung up to open the gate and get his " bawbee." It seemed an undignified way to enter an ancient Cathedral City. After the Disruption of the Scottish Church, the Free Church Congregation had also grumbled. Members from Birnam, the village which had sprung up rapidly after the Railway was opened, could not attend their place of worship without this addition to the Sunday collection, and in these days, when whole families did attend, the addition was not altogether welcome. Besides all this, the toll certainly helped to create and foster a spirit of jealousy and rivalry between two communities which might have been one.

The Toll Gates were lifted several times and thrown into the river during the Riots, several civil and criminal cases resulting. Public feeling ran high. The community was divided. So great were the disturbances that special constables were sworn in and a detachment of the Royal Highlanders sent to Dunkeld in the year 1868. It is on record, however, that the latter enjoyed their sojourn, finding the work of keeping peace a sinecure. Indeed, they commended the community as a friendly one and eminently law-abiding.

In May, 1879, the Bridge was taken over by the County, under the Road and Bridges Act, and the big white toll-gate, so long an eyesore to many, was removed in the middle of the night to prevent any chance of public demonstration.

One of the leaders of the agitation, who fought hard for the removal of the Toll and whose efforts helped largely to attract public attention to the grievances complained of, was Alexander Robertson, a native of Dunkeld, popularly known as " The Chief " or " Dundonnachie." He died in 1893, and is buried in the Nave of the Cathedral, where his name is recorded on the family tombstone.

The Bridge in itself is a picturesque object, and the view from it is justly famous. It has formed a theme for poets and artists alike.

Miss Martineau, the famous writer of an earlier century, suggests that the scene at Dunkeld Bridge should be a particular object with every observant pedestrian.

The Revd. Dr. Hugh MacMillan, the well-known writer and preacher, says, " I know no fairer stretch of a river than that of the Tay at Dunkeld. . . . The views on the Tay for five miles above epitomise all that is best in Highland river scenery."

Another writer, " Ian MacLaren," in his novel " Kate Carnegie," thus praises the view, " But it is so with Scottish folk that they may have lived opposite the Jungfrau at Mürren and walked amongst the big trees of the Yosemete Valley and watched the blood-red afterglow on the Pyramids and yet will value a sunset behind the Cuchullin Hills, and the Pass of the Trossachs, and the mist shot through with light on the side of Ben Nevis and the Tay at Dunkeld—just above the Bridge —better guerdon for their eyes."

Niel Gow composed a tune in its honour and a local poet, Stewart, sang of Bridge and view—

> " Our airy brig's licht arches show
> Five lithographs o' Luna's bow.
> Look frae 't towards Craig Vinean's brow
>   And there's a scene
> Deep mirror'd in the stream below,
>   Matchless—alane ! "

While another bard, Imrie, says—

> " Thy stately bridge,
> The broad Tay rolling at my feet below,
> As from the Mountain Gates it rushes free."

After the building of the Bridge, the aspect of Dunkeld, as it had appeared after 1689, was entirely changed. The long street running from the West Ferry past the Cathedral, terminating in " The Brae," ceased to be the chief. A new street sprang up from the Bridge, cutting across the Main or High Street, the modest Inns were superseded by large Hotels ; Banks and other buildings arose in vacant spaces The Ketlochy Burn, once a bonnie, prattling stream, forming a picturesque boundary as it ran down the slopes on the east side of the town, was converted into a common sewer and continues its course in drain pipes under Atholl and High Streets. The Boat Brae, to the east, then descended with almost precipitous slope to the margin of the river and was covered with whins and broom.

The north and south views from the Bridge present a great contrast to each other. To the north, Craig-y-barns forms a rocky frowning barrier with the long slope of the Craigvinean on its left, apparently blocking the Tay. In the foreground is the Cathedral, grey with years, its green lawn sloping to the river. On this lawn once stood, not so very long ago, the Cottage of St. Adamnan, occupied for many years by the Duchess Dowager of Atholl. The Cottage was a beautiful and interesting object as viewed from the Bridge. Flower beds in front, of varied hues, brightened the landscape and charmed the eye, and the ear was alike charmed in those mornings, gone for ever, when it was the custom of Her Grace's noted piper, George MacPherson, to march with stately tread up and down as he played whilst his ducal mistress partook of the first meal of the day. It was a common sight in the summer to see relays of visitors emerge from the Hotels and line the Bridge as they listened to the strains of music which testified that they were within the "Gates of the Highlands." On the opposite side, a beautiful bank of glowing rhododendrons gave colour to the scene in June. With the passing of the Cottage, and the cutting of various trees, the old building is much better seen, and the sweep of the Tay is solemn and majestic as it comes seemingly out of the long ridge of hill and flows past the hoary battlements and houses clustering on the banks.

Turning to the south and east, the current is broken up into numerous smaller ones, caused by deposits of sand and stones brought down in flood and forming into small islands. Already one has grown so large that it is familiarly termed the Island; it is thickly wooded and blue with lupins in summer. Others are rapidly forming and, if unchecked, will ruin the view in this direction. The prospect on this side is milder, but still very beautiful. Newtyle and Birnam Hills appear to touch as they form Birnam Pass, and again the Tay is apparently blocked, no outlet being visible. Turrets, spires and roofs indicate the village of Birnam. God's Acre lies round Little Dunkeld Church in the foreground, and the War Memorial looks down from the heights at the end of the Bridge. Near what was once the East Ferry is Eastwood House, a residence of the Duke and Duchess of Atholl.

Sometimes, standing on the Bridge, beautiful and useful as it is, a thought rises if, after all, it is an unmixed blessing. It closed the Ferries, two charming trips across the river—no bôats, save for private fishing, are permitted on this charming stretch of water. Inhabitants of Dunkeld have scarcely any access to the noble river flowing past their town. There is a short rough road near the Bridge, a few yards in front of the Cathedral and to the west, and that is all on the west. To the east, matters are as bad. Gardens have risen on its banks. A road between these gardens was open for a time, leading to the Pond, as the town rubbish heap was euphemistically termed. This was closed years ago, though the old name of the Pond is still used, and the rubbish heap removed farther east. There are then three openings in the wall, the 1st, 2nd and 3rd Slaps. From the 1st to the 2nd, the path is rough and dangerous, from the 2nd to the 3rd a clearance has been made and a few seats placed for the benefit of the passer-by. At the 3rd Slap or " Green of the Boat " at East-ferry, the Grounds of Eastwood House begin and block out the Tay, the highroad being kept rigidly away from the river until Caputh Bridge is reached.

Dunkeld Bridge & Birnam Hill.

DUNKELD BRIDGE FROM TOWER.
[*Photo by John Davidson & Son, Art Publishers, Kirkcaldy.*

CHAPTER XIV.

Dunkeld: Its Decline.

FROM being a capital of Pictavia, a kingdom of prehistoric times, and an ecclesiastical capital during the Culdee period, Dunkeld has fallen to the status of a very small Burgh in Barony.

Many causes have contributed towards the decline of Dunkeld. Perhaps the first symptoms set in with the fall of the Romish Church and the destruction of the Cathedral. Although there had been repeated burnings and sackings, up to that time, it had held its own. Its Culdee Abbots and its Roman Catholic Bishops were mostly high-born nobles with princely revenues and kingly powers. Their successors were poor, shorn of lands and revenues, with little influence beyond their immediate neighbourhood.

The pleasures of the chase had once brought kings to the vicinity. It was near the Lowlands, yet on the borders of a wild, almost unexplored stretch of country from which wild animals might be expected to wander, and it had rugged hills of its own and a mighty river; game of all sorts abounded, and sport could be found within fairly easy reach.

William the Lion had a hunting seat near. James the Fifth and Mary Queen of Scots enjoyed hunting expeditions round it. Gradually, as the country opened up and roads were made, sport was found farther afield, and so Dunkeld's importance in this respect also declined.

Scarcely an event of historic importance in Scotland but what brushed the little city with its wings in passing, for it lay in the direct route to the north, armies, traders, and others passing and re-passing it, and it was regarded and spoken of

G

as the key to the north. The town of Perth looked to it as a place which might send warning messages to them when trouble was likely to arise amongst the clans. They referred to it often; " As soon shall the Tay flow back to Dunkeld as expect us to submit to such an injustice! " exclaims an angry citizen in the ' Fair Maid of Perth.'

But if its position brought importance, it also brought trouble, for the march of armies or the raids of lawless men often left desolation in their track. The town and residents suffered from the Irish levies who helped Montrose, the battle of 1689 was a staggering blow, and in later days the '15 and the '45 did not help the prosperity of Dunkeld, for they were incessantly harassed and robbed by all contending parties.

In the reign of Charles II. Dunkeld received an offer which it declined. This was to raise its status to that of a Royal Burgh. The offer was renewed by Queen Anne and accepted, but although a Charter granting the appointment of 3 Bailies, a Dean of Guild, a Treasurer and 10 Common Council men, besides other privileges, was prepared, it was never carried into effect. Dunkeld is now only a Burgh in Barony under His Grace the Duke of Atholl, the jurisdiction being conducted by a Baron-Bailie, appointed by his superior. The Baron-Bailie is ex-officio a Justice of the Peace and a Commissioner of Supply. Holders of this office during a long period were Messrs Conacher and Jack, the latter dying in 1906. The present holder of the office is Baron-Bailie Watson, Deans' Cross, who succeeded the late Mr Kenneth MacDonald.

The Minute Books of the ancient Regality Court of Dunkeld are still preserved among the County Records. Many of the extracts are amusing. Two constables are told off to attend one elder to perambulate the town every Sabbath day during divine worship. What sights would these old stalwarts see could they but return on a Sabbath day! Charabancs and crowds of merry-makers have, as in other places, totally destroyed Sabbatic calm. " Any person guilty of cutting ' cale ' or carrying water ' save in a pint stoup for drinking ' is fined, also anyone found travelling unnecessarily on the Sabbath day." The jurisdiction of this Court was widestretching and the citizens kept well in bounds.

In addition to the Regality Court, Dunkeld, along with Dunblane, was a seat of the Commissary Court for Perthshire from a very early age. The Court was held in the Consistory, or Basement Room of the Tower, and these Commissaries had very great power, under the Duke of Atholl. Illustrating this, a tale is told in Browne's History. Lord President Forbes, dining with the Duke at Blair-Atholl, was informed by him that Commissary Bisset, his depute in Dunkeld, had condemned a man to be hanged. " I am much inclined to pardon the man," said the Duke. The President pointed out that after condemnation no man could pardon save His Majesty. The Duke objected to this, " If I have the power of punishing, it is but right that I should have the power to pardon." And he did.

The Bishops had great power in this respect, too. They were said to have caused criminals to be hanged at Gallowhill, near which are now the Dunkeld House Gardens, and in the hollow beyond sorcerers and witches were burnt. At first the Commissary Court was held in the Bishop's Castle, but afterwards removed to the Consistory. In the room above, records were kept before removal to Perth.

A tablet on the inner wall of the Cathedral Church to the memory of Thomas Bissett, Commissary, who died in 1788, gives a full account of his virtues.

Several interesting items regarding this Court are found in Hunter's Diocese, with a lengthy list of the Commissaries of Dunkeld, the Commissaries-Depute, the Commissary Clerks, the Commissary Clerks-Depute and the Procurator Fiscals— quite a formidable list of officials. An Act of Parliament in 1609 restored to the Prelates the jurisdiction of Commissiariats which they had lost.

Sir Gilbert Stewart of Polcak, Advocate, Commissary Principal of the Commissiariat of Dunkeld in 1661, is mentioned as granting his depute within the parishes of Dunkeld Diocese, adjacent to Dunblane, full powers " for the weill and ease of his Majestie's leiges for putting them to long journeys of wearisome travel in coming to Dunkeld."

During the Commonwealth the Court was ordained to be held at Perth. In 1824 the office of Commissary was merged into that of Sheriff, and Dunkeld ceased to be a seat of this ancient Court, another blow to its importance.

The title of Lord Dunkeld, granted originally to Sir James Galloway, Master of Requests to James VI., became extinct in 1700.

A General Assembly Act in 1587 made Dunkeld a seat of the Presbyterial Meetings of the Church of Scotland, which privilege it still retains. Dunkeld, with regard to parish status, has always maintained rather an anomalous position. It is referred to in a Minute, dated October, 1640, of the Synod of Perth and Stirling, as one of the four " parishones of Lettle and Mekle Dunkels, Logiallachie and Dwillie." In a list taken from the MS. Register of the Assignation of Stipends (Register House) for 1614 and 1615, Meikle Dunkeld is bracketed as a parish with Dowally, yet a document among the Teind Papers in the Register House is entitled " Summondis for erecting the kirk of Mekill Dunkell in ane paroche kirk be the selff and annexing of certaine landis thairto." The document points out " That quhair the Kirk of Dunkell, quhilk wes of old the Cathedrall kirk of the Diocie of Dunkell " was served by the Minister of Little Dunkeld Church and that " it hes not beine ane paroche kirk . . . necessar it is that the samyn be erected in ane paroche kirk to be served be ane minister . . . and that thair be annexit thairto the landis efter specifit, viz., the landis of Tullimillies, Halstones, Graystoun, Blackhillis Drumbowis, Fongorth and Seatt and Haighind." These places are all near Dunkeld, though somewhat unrecognisable under their ancient form of spelling. Since then, whether this purpose was fulfilled or not, the Parish of Dunkeld is often enough alluded to in Presbyterial Registers. Of course, all this trouble came after the Reformation. Before that date, Dunkeld, having a Cathedral and thus being the " Major Charge," did not require a Parish Church.

For a time the Churches of Little Dunkeld, Lagganallachie, Dunkeld and Dowally were indeed served by one minister, but to all intents and purposes the Cathedral has been long regarded as practically the parish church of Dunkeld.

The greater part of the town of Dunkeld was built in the parish of Caputh, which in ancient times formed part of Little

Dunkeld parish. For ecclesiastical purposes, Dunkeld was worked along with Dowally, and in the present day, for local government, it is combined with Dowally and Butterstone.

Whilst Dunkeld still remains the place of meeting for the Church of Scotland Presbytery it has lost the United Free Church Presbyterial meetings, that Presbytery being now divided up as follows:—Two congregations to Breadalbane, four (including Dunkeld) to Perth and four to Blairgowrie.

Thus, with regard to ecclesiastical prominence and importance, Dunkeld has steadily declined.

Another great decline is one common to many other districts. Annual Fairs were of considerable importance, a fact easily proved by a study of ancient charters.

In one charter, dated 1641, it is very plainly stated that the Markets held at Dunkeld were necessary and very useful to His Majesty's lieges. Even long before that date, an Act of Parliament had already ratified to the Bishop of Dunkeld former privileges, and to the citizens of Dunkeld their right to hold a market and public fair yearly, also other fairs and weekly markets.

Various extracts from this charter on the subject of markets give interesting information. " Our Soverane Lord . . . considering how necessar it was to have particulare faires and mercat days to be appointed and set yearlie in the Toune of Dunkell within the Sheriffdom of Pearthe for buying of nolte, horse, sheep and other bestiall and goods accustomed to be sold in the saidis boundis to the great profit and commoditie to the inhabitants within the samens and others resorting thereto for buying and selling, who man be interteaned in the said citie upon their owne expense quhilk lyes in suchane commodious pairt neer to the Hielandis wherefore the bestiall and goodis are and were in use, and customs to come to be sold . . . and siclyke his Maties said umqll darrest father and the three Estates of this Kingdom of Scotland in ane Parliament holdene at Perth, the eleventh day of Junji jm vjc and six yeares being informed how necessar it was to have ane mercat and fair to stand in and about the said citie of Dunkeld at Mertinmas yearlie being ane proper tyme of the selling of goodis to the sustinance of the Leedges quhair ane great multitude would resort rather than to ane other pairt . . .''

Therefore it was granted permission '' to hold ane mercate and publicte faire '' to begin '' yeerlie apoun Mounday efter Martimas Day and therefter to continowe for the space of eight dayes with the haill jurisdiction, freedomes, tholl and customes of the samene.''

It will thus be noted that Dunkeld was recognised for centuries as a convenient trading centre and its Martinmas Market was a lengthy and profitable affair to the citizens, largely attended by all and sundry far and near.

In 1701 the Bailies of the town enacted that '' Pryces in Meal were not to be raised between the two weekly markets.''

There were many weavers in and around Dunkeld and they carried their goods also to this Weekly Market.

In Dunkeld, near the Fountain, the bronze ell-measure gauge, dated 1706, by which measuring sticks were tested, is still to be seen on the corner wall of the houses known as St. George's Hospital. The Markets were great days in Dunkeld. In a book published lately, '' The Campbells of Kinloch,'' the authoress mentions how one of her ancestors used to attend the markets at Dunkeld. He was famed for his courtly manners and appearance, and when he rode into Dunkeld on market days, in handsome attire completed by a Spanish cloak, he generally created a sensation.

MacLean's Guide of 1879 remarks, '' At no distant day, Dunkeld had no less than eight annual fairs, but of these, only Lady Day and Martinmas retain their former importance. Candlemas and St. Colmes are mere shadows of their former selves, while all the rest have been forgotten.''

All are forgotten now. Not even a shadow remains.

The Weekly Markets, too, have disappeared. Friday was formerly a notable day. Then the farmers and others appeared in Dunkeld and then the Gaelic tongue was freely heard in the street, for it is not so very long ago since every farmer from north or west of Dunkeld was supposed to refuse to speak the tongue of the Sassenach.

The opening of new roads, the railway and consequent increased facility of transport, have naturally caused this decline in markets and fairs.

An old record, dated 1729, quoted by MacLean, gives a list of the numerous merchants and tradesmen then, with the occupations followed, which shows how rapidly trade has declined in Dunkeld. There were victuallers, distillers and maltsters, tanners, shoemakers and tawers, dressers of skins, glovers and candlemakers.

The population in 1831 was 1471. In 1921, even including the enlarged Dunkeld Registration area, it only amounts to less than 500, a continual and rapid decrease.

Probably one of the greatest factors in the decline of Dunkeld was the railway. At first it brought prosperity. For several years the iron horse penetrated no farther than Dunkeld, where stage-coaches, notably that to Braemar, encouraged the adventurous to proceed farther. This brought hosts of visitors, who remained to admire the beautiful surroundings hitherto so inaccessible save to the wealthy and the strong. But as years passed, the railway extended, other places also became easy of access and the tide of prosperity rolled by. A new village sprang up on the other side of the river, and then was seen the result of the mistaken policy which placed Dunkeld Railway Station at the distance of a mile with the Tay between. Had building been encouraged, Dunkeld might have retrieved its fortunes then, but as no facilities were granted for this purpose as they are now, the ancient city declined, whilst its more fortunate neighbours shot up with mushroom speed and left it behind in the race.

Dunkeld long enjoyed a reputation for health. This in a credulous age was attributed to the presence of the bones of St. Columba. During a great plague, many flocked to reside in the city. In Sinclair's Statistical Account, he says that the inhabitants are not liable to any particular distemper and many arrive at a very advanced age. It was recommended by physicians for the cure of consumption, owing to its sheltered, mild climate and because goat whey was easily procurable. The same authority gives the inhabitants an excellent character. "They are active, industrious and spirited, distinguished by a frank and open-hearted civility to strangers. No one ever resorted to Dunkeld, whether as an invalid travelling or on an excursion of amusement, without experiencing that they were a hospitable and obliging people.'' This should encourage visitors to resort thither again, especially as new houses are now being erected in beautiful situations.

Many changes are thus seen to have passed over Dunkeld. The vanishing of many old place names, and the substitution of new, have helped to alter the character of the place and banish memories of former glories and events. On looking over old records, the reader is struck first with the strange names and with the numerous '' lairds '' who held their own houses and holdings. Most of these latter are now the property of the Duke of Atholl.

Common place names are the '' Castle Close,'' '' Scots Raw,'' '' Shiochie's Hill,'' '' Balfour's Croft,'' '' Chancellor's Croft,'' '' Prebends and Crofts of Fonghort and Fordischaw,'' ''Lands and Tenements in Dunkeld with barn, kiln and coble,'' '' St. Ninian's Rig,'' '' Tenement of land in Dunkeld called Leacock's Brae or Browster Bank.''

The town, too, in olden times possessed a town drummer and piper, whose dress was faced with blue. A town crier or bellman still rings a bell to proclaim meetings or inform the inhabitants of certain items of news.

LITTLE DUNKELD CHURCH, SHOWING NIEL GOW'S TOMBSTONE.
[*Photo by A. F. Mackenzie, Birnam.*

INVER.

[*Photo by H. Coates.*

CHAPTER XV.

Little Dunkeld Parish.

A T the Cross Roads near Dunkeld Bridge on the south side is a cluster of houses generally spoken of as Little Dunkeld, but Little Dunkeld proper is a large parish covering many miles. It is described in the "Statistical Account of Scotland," dated 1792, as "divided by nature into three districts, each of which would make a parish of ordinary magnitude, stretching from its eastern boundary at Kinclaven to the small village of Invar, then northward along the Tay to Grandtully and westward to Amulree, covering a tract of country containing 31,000 acres." This Account also relates how Little Dunkeld Parish was originally "Dunkeld the Minor Charge"; whilst the City of Dunkeld with Cathedral, Bishop, Canons and other officials, was "Dunkeld the Major Charge." Within the bounds of the Minor Charge various Cathedral clergy officiated over chapels, of which some are not now existent, such as Inver and Inchmagranachan. In time these charges were designated, in old spelling, Letle and Mekle Dunkels. There are various allusions in Canon Myln's MS. to Little Dunkeld. He tells that Bishop Sinclair thought the Archdeacon's income too scanty and joined his office to the Church of Logynallaquhy (Lagganallachie) and "to the Church of Little Dunkeld he gave the glebe which the vicar pensionary at present possesses." In Bishop Brown's time (1484-1514) the Parish of Little Dunkeld was 16 miles long, with breadth in proportion. He therefore "divided it into the old parish of Little Dunkeld and the parish of Caputh. . . Understanding that Irish (Gaelic) was spoken in the Highland parts of the parish of Caputh, he built and endowed among the woods

of the church lands of Dowally, a church, St. Anne, and
gave the priest ground for a manse." Dunkeld and Dowally
now form one parish.

An earlier Bishop, James Bruss (Bruce), appointed to the
See in 1441, was sadly troubled with the Struan cateran
" Robert Reoch Macdonoquhy," who was a scourge to the
church and caused " plunder the church lands of Little Dun-
keld." It has been suggested that it might have been these
godless invaders and not the law-abiding parishioners who are
thus alluded to in the local rhyme so often quoted in derision—
" Oh what a parish, a terrible parish,
  Oh what a parish is Little Dunkel',
  They hae hangit the minister, drouned the precentor,
  Dung doon the steeple and drucken the bell.
  Though the steeple was doon, the kirk was still staunin',
  They biggit a lum where the bell used tae hang,
  A stell-pat they gat an' they brewed Highland whisky,
  On Sundays they drank it, an' rantit an' sang."

Smuggling, of course, was common enough in the district.
The park opposite Little Dunkeld Church still bears the
name of the Stell Park. A more gracious recollection is
that name borne by the park to the east—Ladielands—with
its flavour of ancient church history when lands and churches
were dedicated to " Our Lady," the Mother of Christ.

In the Register of Sasines (fees payable to Sheriff on
behalf of Crown) for Perthshire, 1676, an old custom is thus
recorded:—" Harie Cunison had institution and presentation
in Little Dunkeld Kirk and Meikle Dunkeld Kirk by the
delivery of a Psalm Book to his attorney, Mr John Cunisone,
Minister at Dull, of the ' chaplainrie ' of Invar."

A trouble in this parish with regard to the appointment
of ministers was the Gaelic language. Old records tell of
protests and disagreements when such were appointed who
were unable to speak that language. In 1687, Alexander
M'Lagan (first a schoolmaster at Clunie) was presented to
the Cure of Little Dunkeld, and appointed a sub-dean of the
Cathedral, but as he was ignorant of Gaelic, many of the
parishioners objected to him. He was told to study it, and
rebuked for non-compliance. The proposed settlement of his
son Alexander evoked fierce opposition for the same reason,

but he was ordained and admitted in 1723. The Rev. J. S. Mackenzie, minister of Little Dunkeld in later days, stated " that there was a tradition in the parish that M'Lagan endeavoured to preach in Gaelic in Strathbran; that the attempt was a miserable failure, that he was stoned by the congregation, that at Craig Vinean, near Kennachoil, he solemnly vowed that never again would he preach in Strathbran and that, during his long incumbency, public worship was never afterwards held in the district."

In 1824 there was another disturbance on the same account. The nominee to the parish was unacquainted with Gaelic, and the Presbytery pointed out that it was the common language of the parish and had been used, though not chiefly, at Little Dunkeld and exclusively at Lagganallachy. At the rebuilding of the church, 25 years before, services were conducted in Gaelic. At Communion seasons, there were Gaelic services in the churchyard simultaneously with English, and that nine out of twelve Table Services were in the former language. The case was brought before the General Assembly and many distinguished advocates appeared in it. Advocate Jeffrey affirmed that Little Dunkeld was not in the Highlands, but only " the mouth." Dr. Andrew Thomson's retort, it is said, really won the case—" Whoever heard of a Highland mouth without a Highland tongue," and the General Assembly respectfully told the Officers of the Crown they must find a qualified person for this Cure. Not many parishioners nowadays could follow a Gaelic sermon, not even in Strathbraan.

In the midst of a green park studded with fine old beech trees and laved by the waters of the Tay, stands Little Dunkeld Church, a plain white-washed building, on either side of which is the churchyard. Within the walls, in a small recess near the pulpit, is a relic of the Culdee period, an ancient Celtic bell, of which Joseph Anderson, LL.D., Assistant Secretary and Keeper of the Antiquarian Museum, gives a full description in a paper contributed to the " Society of Antiquaries." The bell is of cast bronze, $8\frac{1}{2}$ inches in height, inclusive of the handle, which rises $1\frac{1}{2}$ inches above the top, and exhibits a flaw in the casting. It is one of four

known in Scotland; one from Strathfillan is in the British
Museum, a second is at Insh near Kingussie, and a third
is the bell of St. Finan of Eilan-Finan in Loch Shiel. Dr.
Anderson accounts for the presence of this Culdee bell in
Little Dunkeld instead of in the Cathedral by pointing out
that before 1500 Little Dunkeld included what is now the
parish of Caputh and that of Dowally. There was no parish
of Dunkeld, and Little Dunkeld was thus the parish church
of the district round the Cathedral. " If," he says, " this
bell was a relic of the early foundation it is quite in accordance
with the history of other known bells that it should be
associated not with the Cathedral, but with the Parish Church
which retained the older associations when the new Cathedral
was supplied with Augustinian Canons, to whom veneration of
Celtic Saints was heresy."

So lightly at one time was this rare old bell esteemed
that it was nearly sold for old iron. It appears that a
minister of Little Dunkeld, the Rev. D. MacBryde, used it
as a dinner bell, and when he died in 1866, it was placed
amongst his effects to be sold at the " roup." One of the
elders claimed it as church property and saved it. It was
afterwards placed in the Antiquarian Museum, Edinburgh,
and was even exhibited in one of the Glasgow Exhibitions ere
being restored.

Another Little Dunkeld bell has also a history. This
one hangs in the Episcopal Church at Kilmaveonaig, at Blair
Atholl. It bears the following inscription:—" W. Glas, min.
lit. Dunkel. 1627." Tradition says that Mrs Glas, wife of
the minister, had presented the bell to her husband's church
when Episcopacy flourished in Scotland. On Presbyterianism
being re-established, Mrs Glas would not permit her bell to
be rung for Presbyterian services. It was therefore sold, or
donated to the Episcopal Church of Kilmaveonaig.

This William Glass or Glas was minister at Dunkeld and
at Little Dunkeld, and he had a son, Thomas, who, after
being Sub-Dean of the Cathedral, succeeded his father 'n
1648. The tombstone of the latter is in the churchyard,
broken and defaced, bearing the date 1682. His son John was

also a minister, and is not altogether unknown to fame, he being the founder of a small sect which still survives.

The Rev. John Glass was minister of Tealing, in Forfarshire, but was deposed from the ministry because of his views. His followers were called the Glassites, although in England and in the United States they were more commonly named Sandemanians, after Robert Sandeman, his son-in-law, and most active disciple. In Dunkeld, where Mr Glass had an ardent following, the nickname of Kailites, common in Scotland, was generally used, from their custom of eating in common at meetings, the chief dish being " kail." Each participant placed a coin, according to his means, beneath his plate when he left. The Kailites in Dunkeld first met in a house near the Cross, but even the memory of these enthusiasts is waning. None remain. Mr. Glass believed that the richer brethren should aid the poorer substantially; those members who possessed property or riches began to feel his Communistic ideas too severe a trial, so the wealthy, it is said, under " specious pretensions withdrew from the connection."

There are other interesting tombstones in this churchyard. The plain weather-beaten stone, with white marble face, marks the last resting place of Niel Gow, Scotland's famous exponent on the fiddle of reels and Strathspeys. It is being renovated and re-touched. Another violinist interred there is Charles M'Intosh, of Inver, noted as the " Perthshire Naturalist." He died in 1922, and in 1924 a handsome stone cut out in Aberdeen granite from a special design by Mr. Thomas. MacLaren, Burgh Surveyor, Perth, was erected over his grave in the churchyard (by public subscription). The long ministry of the Rev. J. S. Mackenzie, who died in 1918, is recorded on his family tombstone, the jubilee being celebrated in the parish a number of years before, and in this churchyard also is buried the Rev. John MacAinsh, B.D.. of Strathbraan U.F. Church, who died in 1925, after forty years of service.

There has apparently flourished once upon a time in the locality a sculptor who had a fondness for Scripture history. Specimens of his art abound in Dowally, Logierait,

Kinloch, as well as in Little Dunkeld. Here is one where Adam and Eve are represented in the Garden of Eden, the former standing beside the tree, one hand outstretched for an apple of extraordinary size. Round the trunk of the tree the tempter twines in the guise of a serpent; overhead is the calm indifferent face of an angel. This same sculptor carved symbols of the deceased's occupation. One stone shows a weaver's shuttle; the smuggler's grave near the church is recognised by the toddy-bowl, the jug and the still-pot. Bullet marks on a stone tell of an exciting encounter with Resurrectionists, who plied a gruesome trade, but on this occasion were stopped by watchers.

On a height at the Cross Roads, almost overlooking the church and churchyard, is the War Memorial. It takes the form of a cairn composed of rough unhewn stones from neighbouring hills, principally Craig-y-barns. Design, cairn and situation all harmonise. No polished artificial effect has been desired nor attempted. On the tablet in front of the cairn is a lengthy list of names, showing that the district did its duty nobly—some families have given three sons and several have given two. A pathetic note is struck in the fact that the inscription—

"Ye are more than Conquerors, who Rest triumphant, Unforgotten"

—is a quotation from a poem by one recorded on the list, Peter Robertson Purdie, Lieut., R.G.A., whose distinguished career at Glasgow University was thus cut short. He was the eldest son of Mr. John Purdie, B.A., headmaster of Torwood Public School, Birnam. The Memorial was unveiled by His Grace the Duke of Atholl in 1921, who then took the opportunity of announcing his intention to gift the ground on which the Memorial stands to the parishes concerned. Several seats and a good path smooth the way to the top, from whence a glorious view is obtained. Just below are beautiful gardens, bright with flowers, bordering the road to Dunkeld Bridge. Beyond is the ancient city, and behind is a panorama of hills not seen from the lower level. The famed Cathedral stands out prominently, with the broad, rolling Tay flashing in the sunlight. On an autumn day the fiery flame of leafy foliage,

the reds and russets of heather, blaeberry and bracken form a
gorgeous riot of colour as seen from this height.   The parish
manse lies in the hollow, and near it is Gowrie House, once
a great coaching inn. Of one of the innkeepers a curious
tale is told. He sold coal, and between two trees he fixed
a beam over which were balanced two creels, one filled
with stones from the Tay, weighing a hundredweight, and
in the other he placed the coal. Nearby is the long, low house
once a school, now a doctor's abode, and in the immediate
neighbourhood, near Ladywell Quarry, is the site of Ladywell
House, no traces of which remain, yet in the 17th century
the family of Stewart of Ladywell was influential, its members
owned the land and acted as Commissaries of Dunkeld. The
old name of " Birnam Falls " was the " Commissaries E's
or Waterfall," derived from this family who were attainted
in the Jacobite risings.

Little Dunkeld Parish contains much that is interesting.
The modern village of Birnam, at the foot of classic Birnam
Hill, occupies the place of importance once taken by Inver,
and then there are Murthly Castle and grounds, full of historic
interest.   To the north-west is Inver, near which are the
Hermitage and Rumbling Bridge Waterfalls on the Braan.
Trochrie is over three miles up Strathbraan from Inver and
may be reached either by the old road passing Lagganallachie
or by continuing on the main road.   One of General Wade's
picturesque bridges crosses the Ballinloan Burn in the vicinity,
and at Trochrie is a fragment of stone wall, all that is left of
the Castle, once a seat of the Earls of Gowrie.   It carries
with it an echo of the famous Gowrie Conspiracy, for William
Stewart of Banchorie, brother to Sir Thomas Stewart of
Grandtully, was appointed Bailie of Strathbraan and Keeper of
the King's House at Trochrie, for services in the " preserving
of the King's Life frae the late conspiracy of umquhile John,
Earl of Gowrie."   Changed are the days since " Grey
Steel," a nickname of one of these fierce Earls, " strode with
heavy tramp while doubting hearts waxed valiant at his nod."
Grey Steel was a chivalrous knight who lived long, long ago,
and it was deemed a compliment to be nicknamed after him.
Farther up is Fandowie, with its Stone Circle and stories of

James the Fourth as a wandering beggar who conferred the lands on one MacDuff in return for his hospitality. The scenery in Strathbraan is wild and bare, growing ever grander as the higher hills are reached near Amulree, on the borders of the parish, and was once a noted ' tryst ' or cattle market. The old song tells that plots, too, were concocted there when lairds and drovers, buyers and sellers consorted together " that nicht at Amulree."

CHAPTER XVI.

Birnam: Its Antiquities.

THE village of Birnam is of modern growth, owing its existence, as has been shown, to the policy which placed the Railway Station for Dunkeld on the opposite side of the river and the distance of a mile from the ancient city. Prior to that date, there were several small hamlets, such as Easter, Middle and Wester Inshewan, and a small thatched cottage, Birnam Inn, on the route from Easter Ferry, was the forerunner of the palatial pile known as "The Birnam." In the immediate vicinity of the Station are rows of substantial houses, elegant villas, an Institute with Reading Rooms and hall, and fine mansions standing in their own grounds. Yet, although the village itself is but of yesterday, it is the centre of much that is interesting to historian and antiquarian alike. St. Mary's Episcopal Church, a picturesque building, stands on the site of one of the ancient Crosses, where pilgrims knelt in prayer when they first espied the object of their veneration, Dunkeld Cathedral.

A charming path through a wood leads to the Terrace by the Tay, near Birnam Hotel, where rise two majestic trees, an oak and a plane or sycamore, sole relics of the famous Royal Forest of Birnam. The circumference of both in 1908, at three feet from the ground, was over 21 feet. They are carefully preserved and propped.

On Birnam Hill also are many objects of interest to those versed in antiquarian lore.

The name Birnam gives rise to diversity of opinion. One Gaelic scholar derived it from two Gaelic words—mam, meaning a rounded hill, and bir, qualifying the adjective

H

" round," as the hill is more peaked than round. Another
connects the name with Braan, the hill standing at the ter-
mination of Strathbraan.   In old charters it was termed
Branen or Brannan, then Byrnane (Shakespeare used this
spelling).   A charter, dated 1644, uses " Birnan "; not until
the 18th century is the modern spelling introduced.

The Royal Forest, which includes Birnam Hill, was gifted
in 1160 by Malcolm, the Maiden, to Duncan, Earl of Fife, on
his marriage with Princess Ada, the King's niece.   This
Duncan was a descendant of that MacDuff who accompanied
Malcolm Canmohr on his march to oust the victorious usurper,
Macbeth.   The Forest was afterwards united to the Barony
of Dunkeld by Bishop Brown, who bought it, along with the
wood and lands of Logy, from King James IV., paying forty
shillings a year.   In 1611, it passed into the possession of
the Abercrombies of Murthly, the deed of sale mentioning that
the turf for thatching the Cathedral and the residence of the
Bishops was dug on the hill of Birnam.

Beautiful as this hill is, with its belts of graceful birches
and green tasselled larches, its patches of purple heather
and green blaeberry knolls, its huge precipitous rocks and
gentle slopes with magnificent prospects, it does not owe its
world-wide fame to beauty or prominence of situation.   It
has been rendered classical by Shakespeare's immortal pen.

Every reader knows the story of Macbeth and great
Birnam Wood.

Duncan, " gentle king," whose assassination by his
general Macbeth, forms part of the play, was a son of Crinan,
the lay Abbot of Dunkeld.   On the east slope of Birnam the
site of his camp is visible, while on the west side of the rock
is a shelf locally termed King Duncan's Bed.   The crag at
which he pitched his camp was pre-eminently suitable for his
purpose.   It is one of the last spurs of the Grampians, and
commands the Howe of Strathmore, looking across to
Dunsinane on the Sidlaw range.   The huge bulk of
Birnam Hill protects it to the north; in the plain below an
occasional glimpse of the silvery Tay flashes in the sunlight.
Seventeen years after King Duncan's assassination by Macbeth, Duncan's son Malcolm marched from Stirling on to

Crieff, thence through the Sma' Glen, until Duncan's Camp was reached, their resting place for the night. Various reasons are cited for the subsequent adornment of Malcolm's army with branches from Birnam Wood. Shakespeare has it:—

> "Let every soldier hew him down a bough
> And bear't before him; thereby shall we shadow
> The numbers of our host and make discovery
> Err in report of us."

An old chronicler, Andrew Wyntoun, has thrown out another reason; he infers that the army knew the witches' prophecy that Macbeth would be safe from injury until Birnam Wood should come to Dunsinane. To quote his quaint description:

> "Syne yai herd, yet Makbeth aye
> In fantom-Fretis had gret Fay,
> And trowth had in swylk Fantasy
> Be yat he trowed stedfastly.
> Nevyrn dysonnfit for to be
> Intill wyth hys eyne he suld see,
> De Wode browcht of Byrnane
> To ye hill of Dwynsynane."

And so

> "Of yat wode ilka man
> Intil hys hand a busk tuk yan."

Be the reason of their adornment what it may, Macbeth's courage fled when from the battlements of Dunsinane, he saw a host appear armed with leafy screens, "And Birnam Wood be come to Dunsinane."

Duncan's Camp, along with the ruins of Rohallion Castle and the Cup-Marked Rocks, all situated on Birnam Hill, in the Murthly estate, form the subject of a paper by Mr Thos. MacLaren, Perth, to the Society of Antiquaries of Scotland, and from it the following extracts are taken:—" Near the top of an eminence called Duncan's Hill, 658 feet above sea-level, are the remains of a fort called Duncan's Camp. . . . Duncan's Hill commands a striking view of the plan of Strathmore. The Camp is roughly oval in plan. Its main access, running north and south, is 80 yards in length. Along the south-western side the boundary of the Camp follows the edge of a precipitous cliff. The other sides are steeply sloped, except at the north end, where there are artificial defences. . . . The south end of the Camp is the only part that is comparatively flat. . . . Stone walls were built by the late Sir William Drummond Stewart of Murthly about 1867, so that the position of the Camp might form a more striking object in the landscape."

Cup=Marked Rocks.

" The eastern shoulder of Birnam Hill, south of the Slate Quarries, is named on the Ordnance Survey Map, Craig Ruenshin; slightly over 800 feet. . . . On the upper surface of a large bench of undisturbed rock which slopes slightly towards the west is a group of twenty Cup-Marks, most of which are well-formed and deeply cut. The space occupied by these sculpturings measures 4 feet 8 inches by 4 feet 6 inches. The two largest Cup-marks are $3\frac{1}{2}$ inches in diameter and one of them is $1\frac{3}{4}$ inches in depth; the others range in size down to $1\frac{1}{4}$ inches in diameter. There are slight evidences of rings round three of the cups, the largest about $7\frac{1}{2}$ inches in diameter. Immediately to the south of this outcrop is a large block. On the top of this detached mass are three cup-marks . . . on the south face also there is a slight hollow resembling another cup-mark."

Rohallion Castle.

" About 30 feet below the top of Craig Ruenshin . . . are the ruins of an old fortalice. . . Rohallian Castle. It lies in a hollow completely dominated by a rocky eminence. . . . It consists of a central block, oblong in plan with round towers at two diagonally opposite corners and a series of outer defences. . . . The walls, which are not more than 4 feet in height above the ground, measure from 3 ft. to 4 ft. 6 in. in thickness."

Dr. Wm. Marshall, in " Historic Scenes in Perthshire," states that Rohallion is called in Gaelic " Forhaillon." According to the same authority, the last time this building was occupied was during the period following the Reformation in Scotland, and it was also a hiding place of William, fourth Lord Ruthven, after the daring adventure of the Raid of Ruthven in 1582.

Between the cup-marked rocks and Rohallion Castle is a rectangular foundation with rounded corners, 46 ft. by 19, enclosing a mound, composed of earth and stones. No evidence of similar formations could be traced in the vicinity.

A green rounded eminence 360 yards from Duncan's Camp is the Court Hill, where Courts were held for the transaction of civil and criminal business. The place of execution was half-a-mile below, and not far off is the place in Roch-in-Roy Wood where the condemned were buried, heaps of stones marking the spot. An oak tree in the vicinity is yet known as "Hang'd Men's Tree," and varying tales are told of the why and wherefore of its name. It is a neighbourhood with no canny history. Near is Honghmanstares, a spot once so desolate that in Notes to the "Fair Maid of Perth," its eeriness is spoken of as "indescribable." Its appearance is now greatly improved by drainage, and the small chain of miniature lakes as the Perth road enters Birnam Pass make a very pretty bit of scenery, the modern Rohallion House being quite near. The skirmish which gave its name to Honghmanstares is alluded to in the "Fair Maid of Perth." The haughty Earl of Douglas boasts to King Robert of his achievement, "When I was entrusted with the lieutenancy of the kingdom, there were some of these wild clans came down from the Grampians. I troubled not the Council about the matter, but made the Sheriff, Lord Ruthven, get to horse with the forces of the Carse. . . . When it was steel coat to frieze mantle, the thieves knew what lances were good for. . . . There were some three hundred of their best bonnets, besides that of their chief, Donald Cormac, left on the Moor of Thorn and in Rochinroy Wood, and as many were gibbeted at Honghman Staires which has still the name from the Hangman work that was done there."

But all, with wide-open eyes, were left staring up into the sky.

There are other versions of the story.

It is said that several Highlanders had killed a Perth citizen and the burgesses flew to arms,

> "And do pursue them unto Honghmanstares,
> In memory of the fight it hath the name,
> For many men lay there, some dead, some lame."
> —From Adamson's "Muses Threnodie."

Any allusion to this place was a sore subject to the Celt afterwards, as shown by the words of Hal o' the Wynd when desirous of insulting his Highland visitor, " I whistle at my work whatever comes uppermost and commonly it is the Highlandman's ' Och hone for Honghmanstares '," which tune had the same effect as whistling " Boyne Water " to an Irishman.

But Birnam has other attractions besides those of historic interest. The walks are numerous and beautiful; many beauty spots have been transferred to canvas by various artists, the chief of whom was Sir John Everett Millais, P.R.A., who resided at various mansions in or near Birnam and introduced their views into his pictures. The rugged shoulder of Birnam Hill figures in one, "Gathering Fuel," Murthly Castle in "Christmas Eve," and many others. There is the Terrace Walk, shaded and romantic, beside the Tay; there is Birnam Glen, following the course of the prattling Burn past the Falls, until the Moor and lakelet of Tomgarrow burst into view; and Balhomish, beyond which through the heather is Glengarr, a miniature glen in length, but with all the magic of solitude, rocky heights, and stream far below the narrow path. And last of all there is Birnam Hill, 1324 feet high, towering over the village at its feet, familiar name to every reader of the world's greatest dramatist.

General Stewart, of Garth, in his " Highland Sketches," observes " Birnam Hill at the entrance into Atholl, has formed the boundary between the Lowlands and Highlands and between the Saxon and Gaelic languages. On the southern and eastern sides of the hill, breeches are worn, and the Scotch Lowland dialect spoken, with as broad an accent as in Mid-Lothian. On the northern and western sides are found the Gaelic, the kilt and the plaid, with all the peculiarities of the Highland character. The Gaelic is universal, as the common dialect in use among the people on the Highland side of the boundary."

As in other cases and places, these remarks are scarcely applicable to the present day.

The hill is not difficult to climb if the path near the Station is followed, and the view from the top is almost unequalled in its panoramic and picturesque beauty.

The huge Bens of the rugged Grampians are here seen sinking down to the wide fertile plains of Strathmore.

As Stewart, the shoemaker poet, says—

> " Here let me pause on classic Birnam's brow
> To look around—land of the freeborn Gael—
> Schiehallion, Ben-e-Vrackie, Ben-e-Gloe,
>   Mountain o'er mountain, rising from the vale,
> Before me now, in rugged wildness, gleam
> The blue hills of the North and Scotland's noblest stream."

On reading the descriptive poem, " Birnam," in which the above occurs, written more than a hundred years ago, there is evidence that Birnam Hill has greatly changed in character since then. The poet speaks of " Communing with the eagle and the roe," also tells that " he who on rocky pinnacle shall stand, shall hear the eagle to the eaglets call." Seldom now is the roe seen, the eagle never.

In a poem on " The Tay," a second writer harps on the same idea—

> " On Birnam's side the light-brown doe,
>   Is grazing by the mossy spring."

In the latter, allusion is also made to the Royal Forest of old and the two trees by the Tay.

> " Huge Birnam towers above the tide
>   All bright with morning's golden glow,
> But scarce a tree adorns his side
> Where forests waved long, long ago.
>
> .   .   .   .   .
>
> None, none of all thy forest throng
> Save yon twin brothers by the tide
> Lives but in tale and poet's song.
> And well it is they have not died,
> For fair and stately do they prove
> Was ancient Birnam's living grove."
>   —Millar.

At that time of writing, Birnam Hill was devoid of trees, but clad with heather from top to base. Since then trees have sprung up, but some who remember the glorious expanse of purple presented in August, regret the change.

CHAPTER XVII.

Inver: Niel Gow.

A MORE idyllic spot than Inver can scarcely be found. One mile distant from Dunkeld, the few houses which comprise it are situated on the Aberfeldy road, just after crossing the bridge on the Braan. Sheltered by hill and wood, its island lawn encompassed by the Tay and its tributary, the Braan, it has several pretty gardens and cottages and is the centre of much that is interesting. Not a mile away is the far-famed Hermitage, or Ossian's Hall, a small building perched on a rock overlooking a fine waterfall. The walk to it is romantic and picturesque, so is the Bridge which spans the river. Farther up is a rudely-built shelter beneath a rock, a "hermit's cave," and beyond this the path joins one of Wade's roads which leads to Lagganallachie and the Ballinloan Bridge. Before this, a branch runs down to the Rumbling Bridge Falls, whose foaming cataract inspired Millais' famous picture, "The Sound of Many Waters."

Craigvinean's long sloping range is easily ascended from various points off Wade's road, and offers grand views of Dunkeld and its Bridge with the valley of the Tay from north to south.

Although but a mere handful of houses at the present day, Inver was of importance before Dunkeld Bridge was built or the railway opened. The Wester Ferry crossed the Tay at this point, and the currents being more favourable than at the Easter Ferry, it was the one generally used, especially by travellers to and from the north. It boasted Inns; a goodly number of skilled tradesmen, including weavers, plied their callings, and it had besides a Meal Mill, a dyer's work and a lint Mill, the latter being converted into a Saw Mill said to

THE LAST TREES OF GREAT BIRNAM WOOD (SHOWING EASTWOOD HOUSE).

[*Photo by A. F. Mackenzie, Birnam.*

be the second of its kind in Scotland, the first being in Leith. In still remoter times, it possessed a chaplain, and emerges from obscurity in connection with the Cathedral. Bishop Lawder, who died in 1481, appointed a chaplain and chorister for Inver. When Bishop Brown died in 1514 the chaplain of Inver was the Prebendary of Ferdischawe, Mr John Stevenson, organist and music-master. Canon Myln thus speaks of him:—" He was a good man; he repaired the old house near St. George's Church, the offices of the Manse he built handsomely from the ground, and tho' he had been often absent from Matins, when he was Chaplain of Inver, by the indulgence of the Chapter for his age, yet when he became Canon he was seldom away."

The chaplainry of Inver was charged with payment of £10 towards the support of a schoolmaster, which charge is mentioned in the Charter of the Royal School, Dunkeld. Before the Reformation this sum, along with others from various prebends, was applied to the support of certain boys called " blew freiris " who served in the choir of the Cathedral.

It is curious and rather interesting to note this connection of Inver in pre-Reformation times with music, for to this day it retains a reputation in that line, and has also been rendered famous by the fact that Niel Gow, generally regarded as the best exponent on the violin of Scotland's music, lived and died there.

> "Old, famous Niel, still many a story runs
> Of his great wit and worth and jokes and puns."

Niel Gow's Cottage, Niel Gow's Stone, Niel Gow's Tree —these are yet preserved and pointed out. Niel Gow was born in 1727. Strathbraan claims to have been his birthplace, but at a very early age, the family must have removed to Inver, where his father followed the avocation of plaid weaver, and there he died in the little cottage on the brow of the knoll overlooking the village. The cottage is in good repair, slated instead of thatched, as in his days, and yet inhabited. At the back, formerly the front, is a large flat stone on which he often sat, meditating, with the fiddle on his knee, composing or playing. Residenters have told of the alarm caused some years ago when certain officials, unaware

of the historic and sentimental value of the stone, decreed its
reduction to road metal. Fortunately the clamour which arose
put an end to the project and saved it from destruction. Not
far away, on the banks of the Tay, is a huge, old gnarled oak
tree, under the shadow of which he often wielded his bow, the
gentle breeze wafting the sweet strains across the river, where
sat listening his friend and patron, the Duke of Atholl. This
tree adjoined Niel's croft, and of this croft a story is told.

One day, whilst working, the Duke accosted him. " Your
croft is small, Niel. Do you get enough from it? "

" Yes, yes, your Grace. The auld meal's no oot o' the
girnel ere the new's in."

The old man who was wont to relate this anecdote would
say in conclusion, " Ma mither's croft wis the next ane.
Niel kent if he but said the word he micht hae got mair land,
but it wad likely be ta'en aff his neebor's."

When quite a child, the future fiddler showed signs of
aptitude at music, which his father encouraged, and several
hints or lessons were received from one, John Cameron, a
retainer of the laird of Grandtully. He soon made his mark.
At the age of 18, he was first in a musical contest and also
had the honour of playing at an entertainment given to Prince
Charlie at Dunkeld House by the Marquis of Tullibardine.
He even joined the Prince's army, marching with them as
far as Stirling, at which point he left, never, however, losing
his Jacobite leanings, as evinced in several of his compositions.

Of Niel Gow's abilities as a violinist, succeeding generations can scarcely form a judgment, but can only harken to those
that have floated down the tide of time; yet all agree that his
rendering of Scottish music was marvellous. One description
by a hearer is thus recorded: " Some men try to give spirit
to dance music by short, jerking strokes with a strong descend-
ing bow and a weak ascending, but his was a continuous stream
of gorgeous sounds, like an organ at full gallop." A special
shout which he gave when changing from strathspey to reel
is said to have given new life and energy to the most tired of
dancers. His playing soon won him popularity, and so
peculiar was his style that no contrivance could avert recogni-

tion. A blind man was on one occasion made judge when Gow entered into competition with nine others. The precaution was useless. " I wad ken his bow hand amang a hundred players," the blind man declared as Niel was proclaimed the winner.

He held his chin on the inner side of the tailpiece, as the portrait by Sir Henry Raeburn, in the County Buildings, Perth, shows. This was common at that period, even in other countries.

His playing won for him entrance into mansion and cottage, and his orchestra was always in eager requisition far and near. Baroness Nairne, Scotland's sweet singer, often tripped lightly to his bow. Lord Lynedoch, the Duke of Atholl, and other noblemen, felt no gathering complete without his music. Hogg, the Ettrick Shepherd, would not have considered his sojourn at Kinnaird House, a few miles north of Inver, complete without a night with the " Highland Orpheus." Burns was taken to visit him, and round the details of this visit controversy has raged.

Sir Walter Scott, in " St. Ronan's Well," includes Niel's son, Nathaniel, in his encomium. The occasion is an " entertainment and masquerade at Shaw's Castle. The audience are becoming impatient when the touch of Gow's fiddle suddenly burst from a neighbouring hedge, behind which he had established his little orchestra. All were of course silent, ' as through his dear Strathspeys he bore with Highland rage,' and when he changed his strain to an adagio and suffered his music to die away in the plaintive notes of Roslin Castle, the echoes of the old walls were, after a long slumber, awakened by that enthusiastic burst of applause with which the Scots usually received and rewarded their country's gifted minstrel.

' He is his father's own son,' said Touchwood. ' It is many a long year since I listened to old Niel at Inver, and to say truth, spent a night with him over pancakes and Athole brose, and I never expected to hear his match again in my lifetime.' "

An Englishman's opinion of the Scottish fiddler's playing is also worthy of quotation.

Dr Garnett, whose " Tour in the Highlands " was published in 1798, thus describes him:—" After dinner at Dunkeld we were favoured with a visit from Niel Gow, a singular
and well-known character, and a celebrated performer on the
violin. His only music is that of his native country, which
he has acquired solely by ear, being entirely self-taught, but
he plays the Scotch airs with a spirit and an enthusiasm
peculiar to himself. He is now in his 72nd year and has
played publicly at Assemblies on his instrument for more
than half-a-century. He has acquired by tuning his lyre what
he considers an independence and which is therefore truly
such. He favoured us with several pieces of Scotch music.
He excels most in the Strathspeys, which are jigs played with
peculiar spirit and life, but he executes the laments or funeral
music with a great deal of pathos. . . . In the evening there
was a dancing school ball at the Inn, to which we were invited,
and where we had an opportunity of again hearing Niel Gow
and to observe the superiority of the Highlanders to our
countrymen in dancing. Some of the children whom we saw
dance this evening would have cut no disgraceful figure on
the stage."

Niel Gow was composer as well as performer, though
well over fifty before his first collection was published. Good
examples of his composition are " Miss Drummond of Perth,"
" Athole Volunteers," and " Lament for the Death of Aber-
cairney "; but in this branch he was certainly excelled by his
son Nathaniel. The latter's most famous composition is
" Caller Herrin'," composed for Lady Nairne's song, and is
a blending of the Newhaven fishwives' Cries with St. Andrew's
Church Chimes.

There are various Gow Collections of Reels, Marches and
Strathspeys, but many are not original, Nathaniel and his
father being " tune-snatchers," often using old tunes, which
they modified, altered, improved, and then re-christened.
Altogether there are six Gow Collections, the last two volumes
appearing after Niel's death, and four " Repositories of
Original Scots Tunes," published by Niel Gow and Sons,
of whom there were four. Besides these, there were other
volumes, one of which, " The Vocal Melodies of Scotland,"

Nathaniel dedicated to Sir Walter Scott in 1825. Nathaniel removed to Edinburgh, where his Band, in which were one or two Inver men, soon became popular. It is narrated that at a fashionable ball in honour of George the Fourth's visit, the King exclaimed, " Gow, you would make the very horses dance." The gift of music descended at least to the third generation. Nathaniel's son died young, but shortly after his death appeared a " Collection of Airs, Reels and Strathspeys," " being the posthumous compositions of the late Niel Gow, jun." In these Collections the old man generally spelt his name " Niel," seldom " Neil."

Niel Gow had also a reputation for wit, and tales of his pawky rejoinders are numerous, " As Niel Gow said," being long a common expression in the neighbourhood.

" It wasna the length o' the road, but the breadth o't," was his excuse when he once put in a tardy appearance, and what borrower would not sympathise with his retort when asked if he had forgotten the pound he had borrowed? " I'd be the last tae mind o't," said he.

One day he was in the boat along with the Duke of Atholl when the latter caught a fine salmon.

" If you caught a fine salmon like that, Niel, what would you do with it? "

" I wad juist send it to the Duke of Atholl with my compliments," came the ready answer. His Grace took the hint and the salmon found its way to Niel's larder.

One of his last utterances was characteristic. Not long before he died, he had sent for and received from his son Nathaniel a new violin. This he allowed a favourite pupil to try. After hearing him play, he said, " Tak' care o't, laddie, tak' care o't. It's as weel worth the money as the thief's worth the wuddie." That pupil cherished the gift to his dying day.

Many of his proverbial sayings are to be found in Drummond's " Perthshire in By-gone Days."

A copy of Raeburn's portrait of him was reproduced as a Frontispiece to the " Scots Magazine," 1809, and there is also an interesting portrait introduced into the design of the title page of the rare work, " Corri's Scots Songs."

He was married twice, and left behind him the reputation of a good husband, father and neighbour. He died on the 1st March, 1807, and was buried in Little Dunkeld Church-yard, where a plain, marble-faced stone marks his last resting place. It was erected by John and Nathaniel, the only sons of Niel Gow and Margaret Wiseman, who survived them.

In the " Scots Magazine," of July, 1812, a couplet appears as an epitaph.

> " Gow and Time are even now,
>   Gow beat time; now Time's beat Gow."

CHAPTER XVIII.

Niel Gow and Burns.

ALLUSION has been made in the former chapter to the visit paid by Burns to Niel Gow. Short as it was, much controversial matter has gathered round the details, several of which, long accepted by local tradition, were challenged lately in the " Weekly Scotsman " and made the subject of a newspaper discussion.

In 1787, the poet, with his friend Nicoll, set out from Edinburgh on a Highland Tour; no light matter in days when stage coaches or horseback were the only modes of conveyance on rough, badly-made roads. Local tradition has long held that Burns, on reaching Dunkeld, visited Niel Gow and adjourned with him to Inver Inn where, on seeing and hearing an irate woman, the poet composed an epigram which he wrote then and there on the window with his diamond pencil. The lines have been often quoted, and even printed, as emanating from Burns.

" Ye gods, ye gave to me a wife, out of your grace and pleasure,
   To be the partner of my life and I was glad to have her.
   But if your providence divine for better things design her
   I obey your will at any time, I'm willing to resign her."

To account for the non-existence of the pane with this inscription, it was explained that, in the middle of last century, the glass was cut out for better preservation and was broken in the act. This version was generally accepted until the year 1924, when discredit was attached to the whole story by an assertion that the epigram in question could not be an original composition of Burns as it was a verse out of an old song-book published before the poet was born.

In the " Works of Robert Burns," published by Wm. Paterson, 1878, and edited by Wm Scott Douglas, the brief

notes on the Inver visit are not of much help in the controversy which arose.   Neither is a letter written to his brother
Gilbert, dated 17th September, 1787, where he thus refers
to his twenty-two days' Tour " down the Tay, among the
cascades and Druidical Circles of stones, to Dunkeld, a seat
of the Duke of Athole, thence across the Tay, and up one
of its tributary streams to Blair of Athole, another of the
Duke's seats, where I had the honour of spending nearly two
days with his Grace and family."

No reference occurs here either to Inver or to Niel Gow.
Several extracts from newspaper articles and letters give
a good idea of the difficulties surrounding the verification of a
supposed fact when challenged a century and a half afterwards.

The dispute arose in this fashion.   An account, based on
generally accepted beliefs in the district, had been published,
narrating several details of the poet's visit to Inver, along with
the epigram in question.   The authorship of the verses was
challenged in the " Weekly Scotsman," Sept. 6th, 1924, by
Mr T. Davidson Cook, F.S.A. (Scot.), who wrote :—" I take
it that here is voiced persistent and little-questioned local tradition.   I gather that local tradition has never had any mis-
givings about the authorship and that the lines pass current
as authentic Burns' verse.   Though the epigram has never
been included in an edition of Burns, the poem has been ascribed to him often enough, and was twice fathered on the poet
in ' John o' London.' . . . Ten years before Burns was born
in Kyle there was a song-book printed in Edinburgh called
' The Charmer.'   It is dated 1749, and there the epigram is
ascribed to Charles Coffey, a dramatist who wrote ' The
Beggar's Wedding.'   Still earlier, the epigram appears in
another old song-book called ' The Hive,' 1724."

This completely demolishes the theory of the Burns
authorship of the epigram.   Mr Cook was also sceptical on the
point that Burns wrote on the Inver pane at all, but the
following letter, signed E. Stewart, a Dunkeld correspondent,
maintains that the poet might have written the verse on the
glass, though he had not composed it.   Other disputed details are also referred to in the letter, so it is quoted almost
in full.

" The story goes that Burns wrote an epigram on the window of Inver Inn, in commemoration of a scolding woman seen or heard there. Mr Cook now proves that this so-called Burns epigram had already been printed in a song-book named ' The Hive,' published in 1724, long before the poet was born. So the belief in the epigram as a Burns' composition must die."

It will be more difficult to kill the belief that Burns wrote the lines on the window pane at Inver, and that this pane was unfortunately smashed 70 years ago. I have spoken to those who aver they remember the breaking of the glass and the indignation of the whole village. The story in this case is that when the Highland Railway was opened as far as Dunkeld, many visitors before and after, came to see Niel Gow's home. The tenant of the cottage at that time conceived the idea of gathering relics of the fiddler into his house as a sort of Niel Gow Museum. He attempted to remove the pane from its original setting, intending to take it to his cottage, but broke it in fragments. It is also said that the same person published a small guide to the district. Were it forthcoming, it might provide information on such points."

Burns' own Diary is too brief and scanty to give much assistance. The notes from his Diary, as quoted in Scott Douglas' edition of his works, are:—

Thursday, 30th Aug.—Come down Tay to Dunkeld. . . . Inver, Dr. Stewart, sup.

Friday, 31st Aug.—Walk with Mrs Stewart and Beard to Birnam Top—fine prospect down Tay—Craigiebarns Hills—Hermitage on the Braan Water, with a picture of Ossian—breakfast with Dr. Stewart—Niel Gow plays, a short, stout-built figure, with greyish hair shed on his honest, social brow, an interesting face marking strong sense, kind open-heartedness mixed with unmistrusting simplicity—Visit his house—Margaret Gow. Ride up Tummel River to Blair.

Saty., 1st Sept.—Have dined at Blair. . . . Dance, sup, Duke.

One night is certainly all that the poet spent in the Dunkeld neighbourhood, and even where he spent it is disputed. Three places are offered locally, viz.:—With Dr. Stewart;

I

Inver Inn; Culloden House, Dunkeld, then an Inn, now the Royal School.

Dr. Alexander Stewart, mentioned thus incidentally, is worthy in himself of more than a passing glance. A connection of Baroness Nairne, through marriage, he was known as the Baron of Badenoch, he being the laird of Bonskeid and claiming to be a lineal descendant of Alexander Stewart, Earl of Buchan, the famous Wolf of Badenoch, whose tomb is in Dunkeld Cathedral. After acting as surgeon in Holland, Dr. Stewart came to Dunkeld mainly through the advice of John, 4th Duke of Atholl, between whom and himself existed a warm friendship.

There is also an account of this visit in a little book entitled "The Fiddler in Scotland," written by Alexander G. Murdoch, and published by Blockley, Regent Street, W. Here in an article on Niel Gow and Burns, purporting to be founded on information partly supplied by Mr Alexander Robertson (understood to be Dundonnachie of Dunkeld Bridge Toll Riots' fame), the writer says that Burns put up at Culloden House Inn, Dunkeld, and saw Dr. Stewart, who, being a keen amateur player, took the poet to visit Niel Gow. Niel played, and Dr. Stewart played, while the bass was taken by Peter Murray, another Inver fiddler, who handed down the account of that afternoon's doings. This same Peter Murray figures in an article, "The Moors," written by Dr. Chambers in "Chambers' Edinburgh Journal," of Oct. 19th, 1844. Dr. Chambers describes an evening spent at Logierait, "listening to the reels and strathspeys played by a clever violinist, Charles M'Intosh of Inver, and Peter Murray, a worthy violincellist from the same place." Dr. Chambers states that Murray, the octogenarian bass, had for upwards of twenty years been the professional associate and friend of Niel Gow. "Old Murray had played with Niel to the Duke of Atholl and his friends sixty-two years ago. He was present on the night when the Duke entertained Burns at Blair."

It will be noted that Burns does not allude to the presence of Gow's Band on that occasion. His sole comment is "Dance, sup Duke."

Another correspondent in this controversy pointed out that the old Ferry House, since burnt down and left in ruins, also served as an Inn at the period mentioned. The house in Inver Square has been generally pointed out as the one visited by the poet, but evidently this, too, is open to dispute.

It will be seen, therefore, that a short visit of one day and one night has certainly proved a fertile subject of discussion. Still, certain details must be accepted. Burns did pay a visit and did listen to the fiddler, who played a number of melodies which entranced his hearer. They were mostly Gow's own composition, and one of them, " Locherroch Side," so struck the poet's fancy that eight years afterwards, when he sent the verses, " Address to the Woodlark," to Mr George Thomson, he gave the tune to which they were set as " Locherroch Side."

Mr Davidson Cook, in his " Weekly Scotsman " article, mentions that this visit might probably have inspired the poet in other ways even if he did not write or compose the epigram in question. He says, " Burns did undoubtedly write a song in honour of Gow when he visited him in Dumfries. Some literary sceptics might suggest that the Gow in question was one of Niel's sons, but nobody knows for certain, and therefore, until proof to the contrary is forthcoming, they are entitled to assume that Niel Gow returned the poet's visit. The text of the song inclines me to think that it refers to ' famous Niel.' " The song is set to the tune " The King of France he rode a race," and concludes—

> " He fir'd a fiddler in the north
> That dang them tapsalteerie, oh."

There is another Gow poem of intense interest, ascribed to Burns, though it has never been included in any edition of his works. Mr James D. Law published it (1903) in an American printed work, entitled " Here and There in Two Hemispheres," p. 164. Speaking of certain manuscripts, formerly the property of Colonel de Peyster—to whom Burns addressed the poem beginning " My honour'd Colonel "—Mr Law remarks, " There is also a poem initialled R.B., and docketed ' From the Poet,' bearing the title ' To Mr Gow Visiting Dumfries.' "

The fact of such a visit is confirmed by a letter which Burns wrote (Dumfries, October, 1793) to Johnson of the Scots Musical Museum, in which he says, " I am much obliged to you, my dear friend, for making me acquainted with Gow. He is a modest, intelligent, worthy fellow, besides being a man of great genius in his way. I have spent many happy hours with him in the short time he has been here."

As Burns had met Niel Gow at Inver in 1787, it really seems more probable that the reference here is to the son, not to the father.

There are five verses in this " American " poem, of which the first and third are as follows:—

TO MR GOW VISITING IN DUMFRIES.

(Tune, " Tullochgorum.")

"Thrice welcome, King o' Rant and Reel
Whaur is the Bard to Scotia leal,
Wha wadna sing o' sic a chiel
And sic a glorious fiddle!
It's but a weary warl' at best
A wauf an' weary widdle;
It's but a weary warl' at best
Gang north or sooth or east or west,
But we will never mak' protest
When near you and your fiddle.

.   .   .   .   .   .

Nae fabled wizard's wand I trow
Had e'er the magic art o' Gow,
When wi' a wave he draws his bow
Across his wondrous fiddle.
Sic fays and fairies come and dance—
Lightly tripping—hopping, skipping—
Sic fays and fairies come and dance—
Their master in the middle.
Sic fays and fairies come and dance
So gently glide and spryly prance,
And noo retreat and noo advance,
When he strikes up his fiddle!"

Be it son or be it father to whom these stirring lines are addressed, at least it was an Inver fiddler who inspired them.

CHAPTER XIX.

Inver: Other Wielders of the Bow.
Charles MacIntosh, the Perthshire Naturalist.

ON the demise of Niel Gow, Inver did not lose its claim to be considered as a place where exponents on the violin of Scottish music still flourished. It retains that reputation to this day. Other wielders of the bow followed the old man, some of them pupils and their descendants.

There were three generations of Gows, but the two last chiefly performed in Edinburgh and the south, and there were three generations of Macintoshes. One of the Macintoshes joined Niel Gow's sons in the famous travelling orchestral band. There were the Murrays, dyers of cloth in Inver, one of whom, Peter, has already been mentioned as having played the 'cello before Burns. Peter Hardie, too, was another pupil who became a well-known player. He was born in 1773, the son of an army surgeon, receiving a University education at Edinburgh, where he also studied violin-making under his cousin, Matthew Hardie. Peter Hardie resided in Dunkeld for many years, died in 1863, and lies in Dowally Churchyard.

Then there was Duncan MacKerrachar, nicknamed the "Atholl Paganini," who on leaving Dunkeld went to reside in Gow's Cottage at Inver. He acted as a Guide to the Atholl Grounds, and was long remembered for his spirited playing and quaint appearance. A delightful description of both is given in Stewart's "Scottish Characters":—

> "Hark, the tweedle-dum!
> That bow hand hath fleetness;
> Gusts o' music come
> Rich in Highland sweetness.

Hearts and heels bestir,
  Rise, my bonny Linny,
Dance to Duncan Ker,
  The Atholl Paganini.

. . . .

A bonnet meets his brow,
  Thrissle-badged an' cockit;
Round him a surtout,
  I' the fashion—dockit,
Short's a plant o' fir,
  Onything but scraggie;
Such is Duncan Ker,
  The Atholl Paganini."

One of MacKerrachar's contemporaries and acquaintances
was William Duff, a fisherman on the Tay waters, in the employment of the Duke of Atholl.   He resided at Polney,
near Dunkeld, and received the nickname of "Beardie
Willie," from his lengthy facial adornment.   He, too, wielded
the bow, was maker of violins as well as player, and was
also a "character" with a quiet fund of pawky humour.   A
life-size representation of him adorns the inner door of the
Hermitage building, placed there after a picture of Ossian
had been destroyed.   Other performers in the district were
William M'Leish, John Crerar and John Sim.   Two sons of
the latter follow in their father's footsteps yet, in addition to
their other callings.   Mr Alexander Sim is a well-known and
skilful violinist in Aberdeen, and has on numerous occasions
displayed his talents at Balmoral before the King and other
members of the Royal family, whilst his brother, Mr John
Sim, was long a member of the Scott Orchestral Band, the
conductor of which, Mr John Scott, Inver, is recognised as a
skilled authority on the subject, receiving the appointment as
adjudicator of Reels and Strathspeys at the Perthshire Festival
in 1924, and, later on, at Edinburgh.

John Crerar, whose descendants are still in Dunkeld, was
a keeper on the Atholl estate, and his features are familiar to
many who do not know his name.   He is depicted in the
picture by Landseer, "Death of a Stag in Glentilt," as looking through a telescope.   He was born near Dunkeld in 1750
and died at the age of 90 at Polney.   Composing as well as
playing, three of his tunes, "Forest Lodge," "The Bridge
of Garry," and "The Banks of the Garry," were published

in M'Glashan's second " Collection," 1788, and the Hon. Lady Dorothea Ruggles Brise, who wrote a memoir on Crerar, says he is probably accountable for others in that collection. He is also credited with " The Merry Lads of Inver " and " The Big Boat of Inver," which were published by Almaine in a Collection of Dances early in the century. He was one of Niel Gow's pupils.

Charles Macintosh, one of the third generation of the Macintoshes in Inver, will be best remembered as " The Perthshire Naturalist." He was born in a small cottage not far from the one which long sheltered Niel Gow, and a neat tablet on the gable end records that " Charles Macintosh, the Perthshire Naturalist, was born here, 1839, and died 1922."

All his days were spent in that small cottage until a few months before his death, when he was removed to his brother's house in Dunkeld. An admirable volume, compiled and written by Mr Henry Coates, F.S.A. Scot., published by Fisher Unwin, London, contains an interesting and exhaustive account of the life, surroundings and versatility of the Naturalist.

In early life Charles Macintosh was a sawmiller, but an accident to his hand incapacitating him for his work, he became a post-runner. The many long miles he traversed on foot while delivering letters were ever full of interest and fascination to this lover of Nature. In addition to his hereditary penchant for music, he had a taste for botany, geology, astronomy and ornithology, studying them to such purpose that he came to be regarded as an authority by those competent to judge. He wrote numerous papers for the " Transactions and Proceedings of the Perthshire Society of Natural Science." One was on a new species of Fungus found at Inver—" Cucurbitaria pithyophila "—and he is credited with the discovery of a number of new fungi. Relics of the past strongly attracted him, and he himself found several stone axes, cists and evidences of the Stone Age.

He was elected in 1873 an Associate of the Perthshire Society of Natural Science. To this Society he contributed

papers and acted as guide when the summer excursions were
in his neighbourhood, besides collecting and mounting specimens for the Perth Museum. His services were freely offered
to various schools, and the rambles of the young folks were
packed with interest when Charles Macintosh pointed out
botanical rarities or called a halt to listen to the bird calls.
Leader and conductor of the choir in Little Dunkeld Church and
Superintendent of its Sunday School, he was altogether a
many-sided man, and in addition he generally filled the place
of 'cellist in the string band long conducted by his brother,
Mr. James Macintosh. After his death, a handsome sum was
subscribed and devoted to three purposes, viz.—A memorial
stone in Little Dunkeld Churchyard, where he is buried; a
tablet on his cottage home; and a fund to provide Nature
Knowledge prizes in Perthshire schools.   The memorial stone,
bearing a suitable inscription, was designed by Mr Thos.
MacLaren, Burgh Surveyor, Perth, and forms a striking
object. The granite is rugged, and on the rough surface stands
out a Cross, modelled on the earliest type of Christian
sculptured stones found in the county. The following paper,
contributed in 1904 to a book in aid of a bazaar for the Endowment Fund of St. Mary's Church, Birnam, shows his
extensive and varied knowledge of the flora and natural history
of the district and also gives an idea of the riches in that respect
to be found in the locality:—

" Notes on the Natural History of Dunkeld and Birnam."
(By Mr. C. Macintosh).

" The district surrounding Birnam and Dunkeld will give
ample opportunity for study. Along the margins of the Tay
the botanist will find a rich but curiously mixed flora.   In
common with the plants usually found by such rivers and
plants common to the district, as the marsh marigold, the
lesser meadow-rue, cowslip, yellow-rattle, etc., are Alpine
plants, as the Alpine Ladies' Mantle, the yellow saxifrage
and the Alpine dock; Alpine Maritime plants, as the seacatch
fly, the sea pink; sub-Alpine plants, as the wood vetch, bald
money or meum, and others, together with numerous escapes
from cultivation, some of which are in the way of being
naturalised; others as the blue lupin, an American plant which

has established itself on the shingle in many parts of the river, and can be seen on the island below Dunkeld Bridge.

" On the wooded or broomy part of the lower parts of the valley the wood anemone, wild hyacinth, chickweed winter green, beech and oak fern are to be seen in perfection. Everywhere the lady fern, the broad buckler and male fern grow in great luxuriance. About the upper woods and moorlands, such as at Balhomish, plants peculiar to such localities are abundant. The lochs, Craiglush and the Lowes, are famous localities for lake and marsh plants, while many rare and uncommon species abound in and around them. The moss flora is also very rich. In the ravine through which the Braan passes between the Hermitage and Rumbling Bridge and similar regions in the district, many beautiful forms abound.

" The Den of Riochip may be mentioned as a notable locality for flowering plants, ferns and mosses. Sad to say, it has been denuded of some of its botanical treasures by unscrupulous and senseless collectors.

" Trees.—In addition to the well-known plane and oak— last of the ' Great Birnam Wood '—and the Parent Larches in Dunkeld House Grounds, near the Cathedral, the noted Scotch and silver firs and other trees in these grounds, there are many notable trees in the district. Around Little Dunkeld, in the Church Park and Recreation Grounds, are many fine trees, among which is a fine example of a plane. This tree, remarkable for its size, proportions and vigorous vitality, stands at the side of the road between Birnam and Dunkeld in front of Little Dunkeld Church. At the parting of the roads to Inver and Dunkeld there is a famous beech, remarkable for the extent, grace and beauty of its spreading branches which in the spring and summer overshadow the highway with a canopy of green.

" In Inver Park the oaks and beeches are large and graceful, especially the group of the latter in the centre of the park. On a bank above the river at the back of the village stands a cedar, one of the largest in the country, which, though damaged some years ago by a gale, is still a fine tree. The Spanish chestnuts by the river near Inverwood Cottage are, if not the largest, yet for length and cleanness of bole, hardly to be surpassed.

" Birds.—As might be expected, bird life in the district is plentiful, both in species and individuals. More than one hundred species have been observed, many, no doubt, being casuals, still the number of frequenters is large.

" Among summer birds the warblers are well represented.

The redstart and tree pipit are common. The sand-pipers, oyster-catchers, black-headed gull and common tern come up the river in spring; the dipper is common in all the rivers and a glance at the Kingfisher may often be had. The gold crest, the creeper, the long-tailed and other tits are met with through all the woods, and in winter they are often to be seen in large flocks.

" The splendid king of the wood, the capercailzie, is now completely renaturalised in the pine forests around, while in like parts, considerable flocks of that beautiful parrot-like bird, the cross-bill, are common some seasons and have been known to nest in the district.

" On the moors, plovers, the curlew and such like moor birds abound, while about many upland rocky parts, the ring ousel nests. The Lochs of Craiglush and the Lowes are at all seasons resorts of ducks, grebe and such water birds."

CHAPTER XX.

James Stewart: The Shoemaker Poet.
David Imrie: David Millar.

IN former chapters references have been made and quotations taken from the poems of one James Stewart, shoemaker, who lived and plied his craft in the Water Wynd,
a narrow lane leading from Cathedral Street to the River
Tay.

James Stewart is one of those minor poets numerous in
Scotland, of whom little is heard, despite their merit, when
their day is past. His name is barely remembered even in
the " wee bit tounie o' Dunkel'," where he lived for many
years, and to the description of which with its scenery and
people he gave his best work. Yet many of his sketches and
poems are worthy of remembrance, if only for the faithful
portrayal of character and beautiful surroundings. While
several reveal the disadvantages under which he laboured,
others show the spark divine. His name is included in the
volume, " Modern Scottish Poets," by D. H. Edwards (1880),
and a short account of him is given in " Perthshire in Byegone
Days." There is also a posthumous collection published in 1857,
fourteen years after his death, entitled " Sketches of Scottish
Character and other Poems." This volume is prefaced by
a memoir of the poet, from which many of the ensuing particulars are gleaned.

James Stewart was born in Paul Street, Perth, in 1801.
His father, a careful, industrious man, was foreman in a
Perth brewery, but probably hailed from Strath Tay, for the
poet's childhood was principally spent with his grandmother
in that district, which was thenceforth endeared to him by

happy, childish memories. There he tells how the quiet, meditative laddie of the Perth streets became the " boundin' wee Jamie that ran daffin' wi' collie and wadna come in." These early recollections were embodied in a poem published in " The Saturday Journal," entitled " Grannie and her Oes," the verses giving a beautiful picture of the fond grandmother renewing her youth as she watches and joins in the gambols of her " oes."

> " Round Grannie the wee oes are forming a ring,
>   What a group! 'Tis like Winter encircled by Spring."

In Strath Tay, too, he saw the Highland shearers pass to reap the rich harvests of the south. This inspired a stirring ballad, " Allan Mac Allan Dhu." At that period men and women walked southwards for days when the cry arose, " The hairst's i' the sooth and fees to be won." Allan was but one of the many Highland shearers who donned " his blue bonnet to rin' wi' the Tummel an' march wi' the Tay."

In his poem on Birnam Hill, Strathtay again has his warmest words. He beholds it from the peak of Birnam, and breaks out—

> " Beloved Strathtay, though mountains intervene
>   Their craggy ramparts 'twixt me and thy braes;
> Yet I behold thee beautiful and green
>   In memory's eye as seen in my young days.
> I see the summer gloaming's purple haze,
>   The pine trees circling round my cottage home,
> The blue smoke rising from the moss-fed blaze,
>   The torrent rushing wrathfully in foam,
> The braes whereon I ran, dreamless of woes to come."

For three years only did he attend school, but in that short time he acquired a fair knowledge of the three R's, and if, as he says, his grammar lessons were few, he must have supplied the want by diligent study. An omnivorous reader, he was familiar with the style and composition of the best writers.

At the age of 12 he was apprenticed to a shoemaker. In later life he loathed this work, alluding to it as his " confounded occupation of shoemaking." Born with keen preceptions, a lover of Nature in all her moods, and gifted with the power and facility of descriptive writing, it was natural that he grew to detest an occupation which kept him chained within doors. Yet, like the great majority, if he did not work, starvation would be his portion, so with his eyes inwardly seeing the purple heather abloom, his ears filled with the cry of the curlew and the roaring of the flood or the sough o' the wind amongst the firs, with his fingers yearning to transmit the thoughts thus inspired to paper, Stewart cobbled manfully at his shoes. Snatching an odd interval, he would hastily scribble a few lines either on paper or on the slate which he kept for such moments in his working stool. These effusions were often left untouched or lost, sometimes given to any who asked for them.

He was twenty-five when he removed to Crieff, where he first became known to the public through a careless sketch. Really of little merit, it caught the public fancy because of the subject.

In the Sma' Glen there had been a smuggling fray in which a detachment of Scots Greys were worsted by the smugglers.

> "Donal' he a' his men drew up,
>   An' Donal' he did them command,
> But a' the arms puir Donal' had
>   Was a guid stick in ilka hand.
> Sae when their sticks tae proonach went
> Wi' stanes they made a bold attack."

Public sympathy in these days was of course with the smugglers, and when they read how the gallant horsemen, Waterloo heroes, cowered beneath the stones they shrieked with laughter.

His love of satire, good-humoured as it was, led him, however, into a scrape with a Highland innkeeper, resulting in his removal to Dunkeld, where he practically spent the remainder of his life. He obtained plenty of work, for Dunkeld still possessed a trade in leather, the tan pits there occupying a yard near the present U.F. Church. As he said himself, commenting on the failing industries in Dunkeld, "Shoon's the staple wark, its weavin's dune." Dunkeld had his best work, for he loved its hills and glens, its streams and floods, its memories of the past, and sought to enshrine them in a

poem, " The Eden of the North," as he beautifully and
lovingly terms our wee town—

> " Embosom'd in a mountain dell
> Like pearl within its native shell,
> As meek as modesty itsel',
>   Retired and shy,
> The wee bit tounie o' Dunkel'
>   Looks to the sky."

> " Do I o'errate its worth
> To ca't ' The Eden o' the North' ?"

Its Cathedral, its waterfalls, Craig-y-barns, Craigvinean,
Birnam, all find a place.   The poem on Birnam Hill has
been specially admired and shows the poet's patriotism and
pride of country.   Looking towards the mountains he says—

> " Here I, a scion o' the plaided race
> Of Scotland's brave and gen'rous mountaineers,
> ' Clasp all these mountains in my mind's embrace '
> With fervid love."

In lighter vein he sings—

> " It's Nature in a philabeg
> O' heather at the Rumblin' Brig,
> Wi' Highland Braan kicks up this rig,
>   Preserve us, folks !
> Dancin' a Hoolachan and Jig
>   Amang the Rocks !"

In 1841, a new vista opened before the shoemaker poet.
A weekly paper, " The Perth and Dundee Saturday Journal,"
began its career and he became a valued contributor.   There
he published a series of sketches, the material for which he
found chiefly in Dunkeld.   One sketch, justly admired and
still remembered, is " Our Little Jock," a true picture of a
wild rattling boy ever in mischief, the despair and pride of a
mother's heart.   The boy in question grew up to be a
respected citizen, John Jack, cabinet-maker, Cathedral Street.
The antics of little Jock amused the poet, so he wrote of him—

> " He's hallacat an' wild, he's gane ower his mither's thoomb,
> He's like a sunny summer day o'ercome by winter's gloom,
> Lachin' like to split his sides, or greetin' like to choke,
> Sae fu' o' fun an' devilry, is our little Jock.

> He winna bide within doors, nor gang to kirk or skule;
> He wore a suit o' claes to rags frae Lammas day to Yule;
> He ran through winter's frost an' snaw, withoot a shoe or sock,
> A hardy, stumpy dumpy loon is our little Jock.
>
> His pooches, like a broker's shop, are crammed wi' orra things—
> Buttons, bools an' bits o' cawk, wi' peeries, taps an' strings,
> A broken file, a roosty knife, an' sic-like laddie troke,
> Wi' dawds o' crimpy, aiten cake, the life o' little Jock.

In a few more stanzas he tells of the lad's likes and dislikes, his martial prowess, "The Queen has ne'er a general like oor little Jock," and completes a picture of a boy who is to be found in each succeeding generation.

Another sketch of his, "The Mistress of a Dame School," is given in the chapter on education.

Meanwhile Stewart was pursuing his daily toil, and in a letter there is an amusing account of his sufferings in cold weather. "I have been striking my harp," he writes, "and I wish to goodness the wires would get red-hot with ecstatic fire to warm my fingers."

Yet the clouds were clearing for him, ambition was soaring high. The "Edinburgh Review," cautious and ever canny, heartily praised his lines "To a Fly Surviving Winter." After apostrophising the "weak, timid insect" which had "overcome the ruthless fury o' grim winter," the poet inquires:

> "What were thy thochts when a' thy kith and kin
> Fell fast around thee as a shower o' rain,
> Or forest foliage when November's wind
> Sings through the boughs his wild bravara strain?"

The "Verses to the Moon," and a fragment, "Morning," also excited the attention of the Press. They are original and the ideas far from hackneyed:

> "Oh bonnily, bonnily shines the Moon
> On her first and youthfu' nicht;
> She seems to the e'e like a rent i' the veil
> That shades the land o' licht."

And:

> "One little cloud, befringed with gold,
> A lonely pilgrim, wandering lorn,
> High on the boundless azure wold,
> Foretells the dawn of summer morn."

His prose style was also good, and there was every indication of future fame and success, when he contracted a cold during a visit to Perth. After a short illness he died in the County and City Infirmary in March, 1843, and was interred in Greyfriars Burying Ground.

His poems were afterwards published by public subscription. The volume is now very rare.

He was retiring in disposition, but full of quiet humour and possessed of such a haughty yet modest independence that it was with difficulty he was induced to accept payment for his first contributions. Carefully neat always in his appearance, one who remembered him informed the writer that he was notably fastidious on Sundays, shedding all appearance of week-day labour, his attire then being blue coat with brass buttons, breeches and broad blue bonnet.

David Imrie.

David Imrie, another lover of the hills and beauties of Dunkeld, also a brother craftsman, was the subject of an eulogistic review by James Stewart, and is an example of the latter's descriptive prose.

Imrie had published, in 1842, '' Scenes Among the Mountains '' (Morison, Watergate, Perth, and D. Macdonald, Dunkeld), a little volume which is now scarcely to be found.

'' This poem,'' writes Stewart, '' is a work of no ordinary poetical ability, although its author happened to be born in ' poverty's low, barren vale ' and bred a humble mechanic. Without the means of a scholastic education and early fettered to a laborious employment, he has imbibed a high relish for the sublime and beautiful in Nature. He has felt the texture of the thunder-cloud and wrapped himself in the mist of the mountain. . . . He has clambered the beetling rock o'erhung with tangled briar, grey lichen, heath and ivy—he has mused in the sylvan dell amidst its fairy mounds, fantastic clumps of trees, green bracken and yellow broom, peopled with the squirrel, the cushat, blackbird, thrush and linnet. He makes the imagination of his reader people the heather braes with the moorcock and the plover, he feels the breeze of the north, he sees the purple heather and the burn that comes down the hazely path."

Whilst Stewart, in this kindly effusion, may have exaggerated the poetic merits of Imrie's work, still there is some literary merit, and it is extremely valuable as depicting Dunkeld early in the nineteenth century. The copious notes attached to " Scenes Among the Mountains " prove that if the author had not a scholastic education in youth, he had overcome that deficiency by reading and research. He mentions the source of most of his notes, thus enhancing their value :—" Dr. MacCulloch's Description of Dunkeld," " Browne's History of the Highlands," " Chambers' Information for the People," " Holinshed's Scottish Chronicle," " Statistical Account of Scotland," and so on.

His volume is simply a glowing description of Dunkeld and its surroundings, with historical notes.

The poem is divided into three cantos, the first beginning with an address to the " Tay's proud flowing stream," apostrophising Dunkeld in this fashion :

> "Yet thou, Dunkeld, thou seem'st my spirit's home,
>   My resting place, my soul's bright polar star,"

and goes on to describe the view from the Bridge, " Mountain, moor and stream," in the midst of which " the ivy-clad Cathedral, grey with years, yet smiles in hoary pride."

Its ancient glories, its bishops with their riches and warfare with the clansmen, " th' immortal Douglas of bold Angus line," are all described, the canto concluding with a wail of regret over the destruction of the ancient edifice.

The second canto is devoted to a description of the Craig Wood and its views. Since this canto was penned the Craig Wood must have changed. A dense growth of oak coppice blocks the way and obscures the path and hides any view. " Dunkeld lies spread in beauty at my feet," he says, but peaceful as the scene appeared, it reminded the poet of days of carnage, so with a vivid description of the Battle of Dunkeld the canto closes.

K

Canto 3 describes walks and points of interest on Craig-y-barns:

> " See yonder Craig-y-barns summits rise
> In countless numbers, like a wavy sea."

The favourite entrance then to the hill, he says, was

> " By Tor-y-buckle's winding path,
> Where lofty spruce-pines form a thicket green,
> Whose outspread branches there in beauty hath
> Formed a fair shelter and a shady screen."

Imrie would search in vain for the lofty " spruce-pines " or " the winding path." These monarchs of the forest have gone—so has the path. Tor-y-buckle is a corruption of the name " Tor-mhuic-geal," meaning " Hill of the White Buck (or pig)," the sounds they make being similar.

> " Still on the winding, devious path ascends,
> While crag on crag rise ever on the view,"

until,

> " High up the mountain side,
> 'Midst rocks and dells, hid from the vulgar ken,
> Where roes and fawns from man securely hide.
> Their homes the hollows of each tiny glen
> Beside the rills that feed yon grassy fen."

The canto concludes with a legendary explanation of the Lover's Leap and the Rocking Stone, winding up with an effort to prove that the great battle between Romans and Britons was fought near the King's Seat.

DAVID MILLAR.

This is another writer who gives a fine description of Dunkeld and its hills, about the same period. He published in Perth (1850) a poem, " The Tay," in five cantos with informative notes. Those relating to Dunkeld are in the second and third cantos. Quotations from " The Tay " have been largely used in various Guides, though seldom adequately acknowledged. The lines on Niel Gow are very familiar:

> " Old Niel Gow !
> There stands his cottage still; 'tis rude, yet there
> The Highland Orpheus piped and laughed at care."

Other familiar quotations are:

> " And there's the Brand! See how it steals away,
> Jewelled with sunbeams to salute the Tay."
>
> . . . . .
>
> " Still could I linger here, Dunkeld,
> Thou old, thou beautiful, thou ever young!
> A thousand memories in thee live."
>
> . . . . .
>
> " Thy little Highland city, too,
> Dunkeld the old, the ever new,
> A bird's nest in a fairy bower,
> Close mantled round with leaf and flower."
>
> " Deeds that were old a thousand years ago."

Millar, too, vaunts the ancient glories of Dunkeld and boasts of Bishop Douglas: " Mitred Douglas, the first in British verse to laud thus Virgil's fame."

Stewart, Imrie and Millar—alike publishing in the middle of last century—form a trio whose writings are valuable to any admirer of Dunkeld and its surroundings. If varying in style and expression they vie with each other in possessive pride and admiration of its scenic beauty.

CHAPTER XXI.

Craig-y-barns: Its Walks.

CRAIG-Y-BARNS is a part of Dunkeld. It dominates the landscape. Dunkeld without Craig-y-barns is not Dunkeld. It consists of a range of rugged heights, at no point reaching the altitude of a thousand feet, yet it possesses, though in miniature, all the attributes to be found in a mighty mountain range. It has streams, waterfalls and reedy tarns, crags, heather and pines, caves, moors and mosses; it has squirrels, foxes and deer, song-birds, moor-birds and birds of prey. This great barrier protects Dunkeld from the biting North winds and forms a majestic background to a scene of sylvan and river beauty. The hill has undergone many a transformation, but it still retains first place in the affections of the citizens. Its contour has repeatedly changed. Bare and rugged when the Highland army, some centuries ago, stood on its rocky ramparts overlooking the town, in later days " from base to brow on crag and dell, waves to and fro, the dark fir tree," and once again " bereft of thicket green and lofty spruce." These trees grew in no ordinary places. They sprang out from rocks apparently so inaccessible that the wonder was where sustenance was found or how they found their way thither. From this circumstance probably rose the fable that seed had been shot into the crevices of the rocks. The trees grew nobly; scarce a bare crag was to be seen until the Great War, when they were laid low, and many a green, mossy path, winding in and out amongst them, was converted into a rutty and impassable track.

Craig-y-barns is cut into various peaks with gullies between, and from this some have derived its name, " A Chreag-Bhearnach " (" The serrated or jagged rock ").

The ascent is comparatively easy, leaving Dunkeld by Atholl Street, at the end of which may be noticed, beside the City Hall, a building bearing the date 1800. This was once an Independent Chapel, then a stable, now a garage. Passing the entrance gates to Dunkeld House on the left, then turning to the right up the Blairgowrie Road, the hill is reached by entering the gate at Cally Lodge, and soon a road to the top branches off to the left, its beauty much spoilt by tree-felling.

The walks on Craig-y-barns are numerous, winding with infinite ingenuity between high rocks, or soaring upwards into dizzy heights. Some are rarely beautiful, beside the tumbling burn, pushing onward through heath and fern. All are varied. They have long been famed, and a fine description, which can scarce be bettered, was written by Dr. MacCulloch, Rector of the Dunkeld Royal School, early in the nineteenth century.

He writes, " The walks among the romantic woods that cover the hill proceed in . . . various directions through the wilderness of forest till they emerge on the open summit. . . . A deep chasm on Craig-y-barns forms a natural pass. From the ease with which the traveller wanders about the whole of this wild mass of rude rock and ruder ground, over chasm and ravine, now on the summit of the precipice, now as if adhering to its face, he is apt to forget, as well as to overlook, the dexterity and the resource with which the extensive work is conducted. He will be unpardonable if he does not examine this piece of rural engineering and wonder at the boldness which could thus dare to imagine a road where scarce a bird could have found footing."

Most of the paths thus described were destroyed recently during the process of felling the trees, but some are undergoing repair. The chief points to be visited are the Rocking Stone and the Lovers' Leap, the way to these at every turn revealing a new beauty. There are pools and burns, rocks and caves, with distant views of lofty Bens, pleasant straths and smiling valleys.

The Rocking Stone is on a peak over 900 feet above sea level, and is a huge mass computed to weigh about 20 tons. It occupies a very commanding position and is raised by

several stones quite above the rocky platform on which it
stands. From this platform the ground abruptly shelves away,
except on one side. As there is no tradition to account for
its name or presence, it has afforded much room for conjecture
and theory. Geologists proclaim it a glacial perched boulder,
relic of the Ice Age, when the valley below lay ice-bound. It
has also been hailed as an altar reared by sun-worshippers,
and a curious fact may be noted that it is placed due east and
west, as if to salute the rising and setting sun. In the distance
the stone presents rather a strange resemblance to a fish—
head, tail, and fins all being fairly well marked.

The prospect from the Rocking Stone is magnificent, commanding a view of the Vale of Atholl, with verdant fields laved
by Tay and Tummel, rising to the great mountains beyond.
On a summer day, no more enchanting spot can be imagined.
The sun gilds the slope of Ben-y-Vrackie or lights up the
misty corries of Ben-y-ghloe, perchance revealing a white
patch, a legacy from winter. Towering above its nearer companions is Farragon, whose bold craggy summit makes it a
landmark and was regarded as an emblem of loftiness and
power.

" Ask the eagle if he can fly over Farragon," says the
proud Highlander to Hal o' the Wynd when boasting of his
own prowess. He could imagine no greater height.

The Braes of Tullymet lie green and smiling, and nearer
still are the fields and heights of Rotmell, for some time known
as St. Colme's Farm. Here once stood the Castle of Rotmell,
reminiscent of ancient feuds, for past it marched the great
Argyll vowing to burn the " Bonnie Hoose o' Airlie." A local
rhyme still lingers, chronicling the fact :

> " The Cawmils are come, doon by Rotmell,
>   They're cursin' an' swearin' they'll burn Dunkel'."

But Dunkeld escaped that time. Fortunately for it, the
present North Road was not in existence and the road to the
east ran behind Craig-y-barns, not in front. So Argyll continued on his way through Glen Cat, past the Glack on to
Craiglush, and through the Stormont Valley.

A narrow path leads from the Rocking Stone to a tiny
sheet of water, heather, mosses and blackberry knolls adorning

ROCKING STONE.

MEETING OF BRAAN AND TAY.

[*Photo by H. Coates.*]

its banks. That insect-eating plant, the Sundew (Drosera Rotundifolia), is very conspicuous in the green spongy moss with its round, red, hairy leaves and small greenish-white flowers. One branch of the path runs round the lakelet, the other ascends and soon reaches the Lovers' Leap, a huge precipitous crag several hundred feet high. The story attaching to the name is lost; tradition is silent, though Imrie, the local poet, has woven a touching tale of the flight of two lovers, converts to the Christian faith, who fled from the wrath of Druidic priests at the Altar or Rocking Stone. Imrie acknow- ledges he has no foundation for the tale. It is a flight of fancy, but may be true. The view from the Lovers' Leap differs greatly from that of the Rocking Stone. The latter looks towards the mountains, the former towards the plain, through the Pass of Birnam. Through this " Gateway to the Highlands " Newtyle and Birnam, giant sentinels on either side, the Howe of Strathmore is descried, the thin blue line of the Sidlaw range on the horizon. To the east glitter the many lochs of the Stormont, and more lie out of sight. Dunkeld Bridge stands out prominently, the broad Tay rolls in grandeur through the valley from the " Mountain gates," past the Cathedral's hoary pile, the clustering houses of Dunkeld, and the more scattered village of Birnam. It is all a wonderful picture.

While the Lovers' Leap and the Rocking Stone are the main objectives on Craig-y-barns, there are other points of interest—Lady Emily's Seat, Lady Charlotte's Cave, the Duchess' Cove—all named after various members of the family of a former Duke of Atholl.

Dr. MacCulloch describes a grotto in a very romantic and beautiful spot, and tells of a man who actually offered to occupy it and act the part of hermit, provided the Duke of that day gave him monthly wages!

Imrie, writing at a later period, says the grotto known by the name of the Duchess' Cove was a favourite resort; " here throwing aside the pomp and grandeur of her station, it was said she would ply the wheel for hours, attended only by some worthy domestic. Nor did his Grace ever fail to pay his Duchess a visit in her solitary bower, where a repast, usually some dainty of the season, was spread, which they enjoyed.''

Imrie also mentions that in his time the grotto was in a very dilapidated state. It is more so now.

Just below the Lovers' Leap there is another neglected spot, once trim and beautiful, where still flourish rhododendrons and other shrubs. Locally this is MacRaw's Garden, but MacCulloch's Guide terms it Lios-na-craggan (The garden of the rock), it being then an ornamental enclosure teeming with rich flowers. Before that period, however, there was a cottage with garden attached, tenanted by a worthy and industrious couple, David and Janet MacRaw. Looking at the wilderness it now presents, it is surprising to read in old books of the fruit, flowers and potatoes grown there. David's employment was to keep the walks in repair and to see no damage was done to young trees. His wife sold to visitors strawberries and cream, '' bread of her own baking, cheese of her own making.'' An old rhyme runs :

> " In Craig-y-barns there lived a pair,
> Far frae strife, and free from care;
> But death cam' rapin' to their door,
> An' sent them to Dunkeld, O."

They died in 1805 and rest in Dowally Churchyard.

At the base of the hill are two small lochs, a mile or so apart, Cally and Polney—often spelt '' Pulney,'' but the former is said to be the correct designation. Cally, once a peat moss in use, was laid out beautifully with foreign shrubs on its banks and water lilies on its surface. Round it went a broad green walk, '' where soft the footstep falls,'' but the loch at this day is weedy and neglected and rush-grown, its soft mossy paths cut up and piles of broken timber covering the shrubbery. Yet in May or June the red masses of rhododendron and the yellow bloom of azaleas hide much that is unsightly; again in autumn the crimson colouring of azalea leaves and the varied tints of other plants resemble a tropical scene in their fiery flame of colour.

Polney lies close to the Pitlochry road, exactly one mile from Dunkeld, with the rocks of Craig-y-barns rising nobly

Reflections Loch Pulney, Dunkeld.

REFLECTIONS ON POLNEY.
[*Photo by John Davidson & Son, Art Publishers, Kirkcaldy.*

behind. The correct nomenclature of this small loch is Pol-nan-Geadas, meaning the " Pike pool," that fish being in abundance in its waters. It is a romantic spot; votaries of the " roarin' game " frequent it in winter, and many a shout has echoed along its banks. Close by is the King's Pass, with the King's Seat on the left, within the Dunkeld House policies, as are the " Standing " and " Early Christian " Stones already described. Another Stone, but in the Tay, is not far off and bears a curious name. This is the Clach-na-Taggart, or " The Priest's Stone "; a few smaller stones are so placed in the water as to form a crossing to it from the bank.

In the King's Pass, but on the right-hand side of the road, is another of the Craig-y-barns caves. Duncan Hogg's Hole is high up amongst the precipitous rocks. Duncan was a free-booter in the good old times and lived by plundering or reliev-ing travellers of their goods, but the date of his doings is unregistered.

Craig-y-barns is rich in natural history. One poet sings :

> " Round Craig-y-barns' clifty brow,
> The goshawk wheels on moveless wings ";

Another :

> " And there, see, roond by Craig-y-barns,
> The corbies sail."

The roe and the fallow deer have their haunts in its re-cesses, though the former are not so numerous as they were ; the fox is occasionally seen ; the capercailzie is at home in its fir trees, so is the kite. Once the golden eagle nested on its crags, the polecat was a dangerous tenant, and the wild goat found footing on its narrowest ledges. The early Kings of Scotland found the hunting of boars and other wild animals attractive enough to bring them often to the vicinity. William the Lion is said to have had a hunting seat on the detached portion which thus bears the name of King's Seat. At the foot is a well named St. Columb's Well.

CHAPTER XXII.

" Grews Well " and Surroundings.

VIEWING the north-east from Craig-y-barns, the beholder sees a wild stretch of hilly country, in which there lies, secluded and desolate, a tiny roadside spring, once of more than local fame. This is the Grews Well, about six miles from Dunkeld. Many, many years ago, long before the Reformation, a chapel was erected there for the benefit of those who spent summer in the shielings, tending their cattle and watching their flocks. Tradition and legend still busy themselves round the origin and fame of this Well. One tradition affirms that here a holy man retired from the world to meditate and pray in solitude. He used the pure water of the spring, and his use sanctified it. Another story finds in the proximity of the chapel a plea for the sanctity of the Well. It was the Well of the Holy Cross—Sancta Crux or Cruz—softened in local nomenclature to Grews Well. Whatever the reason, it was regarded as a Wishing Well and a Well which cured all diseases. Numerous indeed are the tales which circle around the Well.

Its fame is not confined to the immediate district. Thousands from all parts flocked to it in Roman Catholic times, arriving halt and maimed, returning sound in mind and body; the font in use then, a rude stone basin, survives and still remains in the overflow streamlet, set around with moss, heather and bog myrtle. But to find the cure truly efficacious the sufferer must journey thither on the first Sunday of May (Old Style is generally reckoned yet) and this points to the probability of the annual pilgrimage being actually a relic of Pagan times, a Beltane feast, when the people assembled to welcome summer and to watch the kindling of the fire of Baal.

This Well figures in the Presbyterial Records of Dunkeld at least as far back as 1656. The Assembly about that period were greatly exercised as to witchcraft, and special efforts were made to fight the supposed evil. Perthshire had not been exempt from the terrors of witchcraft in the past. Margret, Countess of Atholl, was alleged to have been guilty of witchcraft in 1566 (Laws' Memorialls), and in 1570 witches in Atholl were said to have sent a present to Queen Mary. It was a pretty hart horn, the size of the palm of a man's hand, covered with gold. On it were engraven the Arms of Scotland, with a gentlewoman seated on a throne with a crown on her head. The rose and thistle were under her feet. Below were two lions and the motto, " Fall what may fall, the lyon sall be lord of all." (Calderwood's History). So it behoved the Presbytery to be zealous; " charmers " were suspected of paction with the evil one. On April 27, 1656, the elders of Logierait were " exhorted to be circumspect in their places that none goe to wells and especiallie John Robertsone at the Porte to take notice of any that goes that way to Crewss Well."

Another extract from the Rattray Kirk Session Minutes, Aug. 30, 1657, reads, " Compaired Christiane Reat who was accused of breach of Sabbath by travelling thereon to Grwss Well and for ascribing more vertew to that Well upon that day (the first Sabbath of May) nor to any other well upon any other day." Poor Christian pleaded that she only did as others did, but " the Minister did labour to make her sensible that it was sinfull to hir to doe such things, and she submitted hirself to the will of the session." The following Sabbath she had to confess her sin publicly and promise never to do the like again.

Still, the belief in the healing powers of the Well persisted, and as recently as 1842, Imrie records in his " Notes ": " This spring, Grews Well, is considered to possess medicinal qualities of the first order, but the only time that these qualities have their proper efficacy is on the first Sabbath of May, Old Style. Annually upon that day, many still resort to that spring travelling sometimes twenty and even thirty miles fully convinced that the drinking of the water and other ceremonies will restore health when all other remedies have failed. But the drinking of the spring is not all, there are certain stones of the place which must be used also; there is one for almost every disease and there is always some person on the spot to point out the proper stones and give instructions how they are to be used. . . . Everyone who expects to be benefited must put something into it for an offering; small pieces of money used to be dropped in, but now only buttons or pins. It is stated that those who take out offerings never thrive, but it appears that it has been often risked. Immediately above the Well is a Cairn that has also to be traversed three times round and a stone added."

There are various ways of reaching the Well from Dunkeld. One, passing the Fungarth Knowes and Craiglush, leaves the Blairgowrie Road shortly after the third milestone, the Cardney Burn on the left, and reaches Grews Well by way of Knowehead and Over Cardney; another leaves the same road about a mile farther on, near Butterstone, climbing upwards through the romantic Den of Riechip. The most picturesque, however, is that which passes through the gate at Cally Lodge. This latter route is wild and solitary. Skirting Craig-y-barns and the Piper's Moss, the road passes Cally Loch, Upper Hatton and Birkenburn; thence through the " Glack " or " gap," once a foxhunting place, on to the Chapman's Brig—a name recalling pedlar days. Rumour has it that one of these worthies hanged himself at this spot. Silent and solitary, eerie even, as this path is, it leads through a district which was once populous and cultivated. In old records, references are made to many of the places close at hand, which are but heaps of stones dotted on marsh or heathery moorland; the only sound to break the silence, the cry of moorland birds. Such are Craigilto or Auchagowan. Yet corn once ripened there, cattle and poultry fattened, for in a church record, dated 1674, we read that the proprietors, tenants and others gave, or were asked for, the tenth sheaf of corn, the tenth stone of cheese, the tenth goose or calf, and such like products. The lands belonged then to the Church, and certain rights and privileges connected with them were granted to the citizens of Dunkeld by the Bishop, 1641, places mentioned being the " Haltowne

of Tulliemille, Auchnagoule and Birkerburn.'' Spelling was
not a strong point long ago. From these places, too, came
weavers to sell their wares in Dunkeld market; and a stone
near the Hatton, which was but lately broken up, was known
as " Lang tow,'' receiving this designation from the nickname
of a weaver, famed for his height, who, toiling to the weekly
market at Dunkeld with his wares, invariably rested on its
flat surface.

From Chapman's Brig a glorious view over the hills is
obtained. Farther on is the Leddoun Crag and Gate. Above
rises precipitously the rocky, riven heights of the Deucharie,
a few years ago crowned with firs, its sides purple with heather.
It rises shorn of its glory; the firs have fallen and the heather
has yielded to the insidious advance of bracken.

This road, or part of it, figured in a right-of-way case
which created much excitement at the time. It had long been
regarded by many as an indisputable right-of-way, and when
several incidents occurred which seemed likely to deny that
assumption, contention arose. After various preliminaries
and much heated dispute in the Dunkeld Parish Council, the
County Council refused to take the matter up. A Dunkeld
Public Rights Committee was formed, and of these, three
acted as pursuers in the case. It was tried in the Court of
Session before the Lord Justice-Clerk, Edinburgh, March,
1906, the Press giving a very full report of the proceedings.
The pursuers' case was that there was a right-of-way from
Dunkeld to Kirkmichael, leaving the public highway at Cally
Lodge, thence by the Hatton, Birkenburn, Glack, Cardney
Hill and Grews Well. The defenders contended that the roads
in question were estate roads on the Atholl and other estates.
Many witnesses were called for and against. After long de-
liberation, the jury found unanimously that the pursuers had
failed to establish their claim, the Lord Justice-Clerk, in
summing up, laying stress not on the number of people who
had used the road believing it to be a right-of-way, but on
the point that there had been a fence, unchallenged, across
part of it for many years. The decision was somewhat in the
nature of a surprise to many.

The district is a network of old roads, relics of bygone days, bridle paths and drove roads.

The track joins the Butterstone Road not far from a house, dismantled but not yet quite in ruins, and opposite it is the Well, just beneath the bank. Still to be seen, moss-grown and under grass it is true, and half-hidden yet conspicuous enough to the observant, are the special stones for backache, toothache or headache. Buttons or crooked pins ornament the sandy soil in the Well, offerings of a sordid age; though there are pilgrims yet who aver there is virtue in the Well.

One witness in the right-of-way case referred to, said he was taken there as a child for the whooping-cough. Another declared he had heard of a man who was taken there on a barrow and jumped out himself. A third witness told how he took his child there himself and made her wash in the water, as the doctor had said he could do no more. Either the bathing or change of air did her good, and he had also heard of a man who was carried there, who bathed and then walked home.

Other places of interest are in the vicinity. The three high hills which look down upon the Well, the Deucharie, Ben-e-challie and Riemore, have all glorious views of fertile plains, moors and mountains, lochs and rivers, villages and towns, and clumps of white heather are wonderfully common.

Ben-e-challie (1594 feet high) is recognised by the tower on its top, locally alluded to as " Lazy Donald." The story is told that when the men employed by Sir John Bissett of Riechip were digging the foundation for this tower, they came across a skull, bones, brass buttons and accoutrements which indicated a trooper's dress. The supposition was that a messenger journeying northwards from Perth to Braemar with money to pay troops was murdered for its sake. In the Den of Riechip near by is the " Murderer's Well."

The view from the top is very extensive. It looks towards Birnam on the south with Deucharie rising darkly on the north, its position betwixt the two giving rise to a weather rhyme :

> " Ben-e-challie says to Deucharie,
> Birnam's got a tap;
> Deucharie says to Ben-e-challie,
> Then we'll hae a drap."

This saying is seldom, if ever at fault, for mist on Birnam is a sure precursor of rain.

In the hill are two caves. One, " Harry's Hole," whither " Harry " retired after forcing the unwary passer-by to pay tribute; and the " Drap," the latter recognised when found by the reiterated, constant sound of a drop of water.

The view comprises the Sidlaws, the Fife Lomonds, with the wilder Grampian peaks as Schiehallion, Ben Lawers, Ben-y-ghloe and mountains beyond Glenshee, while a unique feature is the large number of lochs visible. At the base, Ben-e-challie Loch yields its waters to supply Blairgowrie, and Loch Ordie gives to Dunkeld. Many of the Stormont lochs sparkle in the valley, Clunie with its ancient Castle and Island forming a picture in itself.

From the hill of Deucharie other lochs appear, amongst them the tiny pear-shaped Loch Oiseannachd, near which the famous divine, Robert Murray M'Cheyne, once spent a night wrapped in his cloak, having lost himself walking from Dunkeld to Kirkmichael. The old drove road to Kirkmichael winds along the side of Riemore, and a mile or two up is the Cross o' Coupar. On an Ordnance map this was marked B.S., or Boundary Stone, and is, or was, similar in shape to a milestone, sloping on the top. A strange place for such a stone, it may appear, with brooding silence and solitude all around, but once upon a time a different tale might be told. The stone marks the boundary of the Abbey Lands of Coupar; there were several of such marks; at the Chapman's Brig was another. A market was also held at one time at the Cross o' Coupar; farmers and drovers congregated there as a central spot and there is a park in the neighbourhood still called " The Drovers' Park." Stretching away for miles is the Forest of Clunie, a sight to sadden any lover of Scotland, for in the graphic words of a Perthshire farmer, " Once forty smokes ascended, now there is but one." There are no stories of eviction. People appear to have just drifted away.

About a mile beyond Grews Well is Loch Ordie. At an altitude of nearly a thousand feet, it lies in an ampitheatre of lonely hills. A few short years ago, bosky glades of fir and fern adorned its banks. Scarcely a tree remains. The Loch Ordie plantations were famous in their day. A curious account of the planting, begun in 1815, is narrated in MacLean's Guide. The purchase of several thousands of acres of ground at 25 years' purchase was 9d. per acre per annum. The plants cost 4/- per 1200, the expense of roads, drives and bridges was only 7/6 per rood, men's wages each 1/3 per day, and the expenditure altogether £2 10/- per Scotch acre.

In the same Guide a quotation occurs from a letter written by John, 4th Duke of Atholl, with regard to this plantation. He writes : " Drove up to Loch Ordie and home by the back of Craig-y-barns, very much gratified by the growth of larch and the spruce. A very fine, grand, picturesque drive, not to be equalled in Britain. The extent of the drive through woods of my own planting, from one to forty years old, is fifteen miles."

The Royal Navy, the Mercantile Marines and the rail-roads of Britain have benefited by such plantations. For one frigate alone, " The Athole," built in 1816-20, 772 larches were cut down between Dunkeld and Blair-Atholl.

The banks of Loch Ordie are again bare, but there still remains the witchery of sparkling waters and the exhilaration of mountain air. The loch itself is about 2½ miles in circumference and has a peculiar outcrop rock and numerous pretty little bays and creeks. At one end is a Cairn commemorating the visit of Queen Victoria.

CHAPTER XXIII.

The Lochs: Craigrankie.

LOCHS are numerous in the Dunkeld district, but when the Lochs, pure and simple, are mentioned, everyone understands that those referred to are the three at the entrance to the Stormont valley, connected with half-a-dozen others, lying in the route to Blairgowrie. The Loch o' the Lowes, Craiglush and Butterstone are all romantically beautiful, and within easy walking distance of Dunkeld. The first-named is the largest and nearest, barely two miles off. It can be reached either by highway or by charming by-ways. A favourite one begins by climbing the steep street in Dunkeld termed by residents The Brae. On the last house to the right, but a little way off and turned sideways, is the quaint Sundial dated 1757, with the names of John Ballantyne and Jaunet Stewart; the experience of the former in the '45 has already been narrated in Chapter IX.

Continuing the steep ascent, there is a very fine view, almost Continental in aspect, looking back on the street, with the houses unequal in height as they ascend, the rest of Dunkeld clustering in the hollow, hills beyond and peeps of the noble bridge spanning the Tay. A few large houses are built on the plateau at the top, and the road runs along by the Craig Wood. A small walled enclosure in a field to the right often excites comment. This is the site of an old chapel, once called the Red Chapel, dedicated to St. Jerome and built for the use of the inhabitants of Fungarth, who long retained the nickname of the " Funnart Jorums." If one looks closely a track running up the side of the wood leading towards Fungarth can still be discerned. Near this, on either side of the road are two grassy patches of ground, sole relics of the

L

old common, where drovers rested their sheep and cattle on the way to market, this being originally a high road to Dunkeld. A few old trees on the right gave the name of "The big trees" to the spot, but the largest fell many years ago.

The road to the Lowes here branches to the left, passing Haughend Farm on the right and skirts the Craig Wood and Craigrankie by one of the most beautiful walks in a beautiful neighbourhood. It should be seen in the months of May and June, when the misty, smoky blue of the wild hyacinth in its masses forms a never-to-be-forgotten sight. Craigrankie and Newtyle Hill rise to the right, the former covered with bracken and blaeberry, the latter lately planted, chiefly with larch. The views from the top of these hills are very pretty, including the Stormont valley and lochs, the Sidlaws and Strathmore, the Dunkeld valley, river and bridge, Strathbraan, and on a clear evening the houses and chimney stalks of Perth stand out quite plainly. This climb up Craigrankie past heather clumps, blaeberry knolls and burns is one of the easiest and prettiest near Dunkeld. Only the plaintive call of the feathered denizens of the upland moor or the distant bleating of sheep may break the silence. Occasionally the deer may be seen bounding away, while from hill and moor blows the life-giving breeze, keen and exhilarating. Crossing the Dean's Burn, the top of Newtyle is reached; it is known as the Teetotaller's Seat, though history is silent as to the reason why. In a corner amongst the rocks on this hillside is the "Weaver's Kirk," where in olden days several of that fraternity met on the Sabbath to discuss matters of deep moment. Right below is Dean's Cross. Here was the site of one of the Crosses placed by a pious Dean for the benefit of those pilgrims who sought Dunkeld Cathedral, because at this point they obtained their first glimpse of that sacred edifice. Doubtless these same pilgrims offered up a prayer of fervent thanksgiving when they arrived at the Cross in safety, for on Stenton Rock, a mile behind, lived the notorious freebooter, Kemp, who lay in wait to relieve them of their intended offerings to the Church.

Another version of the name, however, is Danes' Cross, which is explained by saying that the Danes crossed the Tay in this vicinity. In a deep pool, too, near this, it is alleged that witches were wont to find a watery grave. Along the base of the hill is a path or old church road between Clunie and Caputh, still called the People's Walk. Winding round Haughend Farm it emerges on the Caputh road at what was once the hamlet of Woodhead, Only a few stones are left to testify to the presence of a former "hamlet grey." In the burn beside it the inhabitants used to steep their lint. On the opposite side is a wood with little dells sloping towards the Tay. One of these in the spring is so yellow with primroses that the children loved to wander and "pluck the primrose gay." They named it "the primrose dell," but the little hands will touch the yellow petals there no more, for it is now enclosed ground and fenced off.

Returning to the Lowes path, Fungarth with its Golf Links comes into view. In old writings Fungarth has various spellings—Fonghort, Fongoarth, Fingorth or Fungorth are all used—and it boasted a Prebendary in connection with the Cathedral. One of the hollows is named the Highlandman's Howe, and there the Dunkeld Games were once held.

Ere long the Loch o' the Lowes comes into view, and is soon reached. It is about three miles in circumference and is very beautiful; a fine sheet of water nestling among the hills, a gem of beauty set in emerald, thickets of birch, alder and wild roses. Unfortunately, alders and hazel in their overgrown profusion threaten to obscure the views and hide the loch. The encroachment of such shrubs is also tending to destroy the botanical riches of the banks. Wild thyme, bog myrtle, meadow sweet and heather each perfumes the air in its season; the butterfly and other species of orchis are common, and blue lobelia, with other varieties of water plants, adorn the surface of the loch. Water birds are numerous; wild duck and water hen here nest, plovers, curlews, snipe and sandpipers abound. In the autumn brambles are plentiful on the banks and meadows near. At the east end of the loch a building once stood made useful for hunting operations. Here was the rendezvous for the boar hunt, and here the hounds were unleashed or "lowsed." Hence the name of "Loch o' the Lowes," although there is another explanation given—Loch o' the Pikes—in this case "Lowes" being a corruption of lucius, Latin for pike, a name probably used by the priests of old.

There are several roads round about the loch. One, with fascinating peeps of the water, passes the Letter and the Lowes Farms, through the Pow, runs alongside Butterstone Loch and joins the Blairgowrie Road near Butterstone. The main road turns up by Catchpenny, Craig-en-taggart, Snaigow on to Clunie, where it, too, sends a branch to the Blairgowrie Road or continues to the end of Clunie Loch. This latter loch is more pastoral in character than the Loch o' the Lowes, but it is quietly pretty and picturesque with its island and ancient Castle, once the " Key of the See of Dunkeld." It is also rich in historical associations. Before the Castle was built, 400 years ago, by Bishop Brown of Dunkeld, there was a stronghold occupied by a gang of robbers, who sacrilegiously carried off the fruits of the earth or pious offerings brought by parishioners from Alith to Dunkeld. The good Bishop succeeded in rooting them out, and used the Castle as a summer residence. Worn out with sorrow, sickness and the worry of controlling the stormy factions of the period, he died here in 1514.

The Castle was also the home, if not the birthplace, of the " Admirable Crichton," an account of whom is given in Chapter VI. Close to the loch is a large green mound called the Castle Hill, on which traditions says was erected the Summer Palace and Hunting Seat of Kenneth MacAlpin, first King of the Picts and Scots. The Danes were defeated by him in 845 in the neighbourhood.

Clunie is about four miles from Blairgowrie, the road passing the remainder of the lochs, there being nine altogether in the Stormont, which is a wide, fertile vale bordered by pastoral and also rugged hills. The name is said to mean " main battle or strife," and on this derivation is founded the idea that somewhere in the valley was fought the great battle between Romans and Britons.

Returning to Dunkeld by Forneth, the Laighwood and Butterstone, there are many objects of interest, amongst them the remains of Pictish dwellings. Just above Butterstone village is the Cloven Stone, cleft in two, an opening several inches wide between each. It closed by using a lever, each part fitting into the other, and weighs at least ten tons. From Butterstone, through the romantic ravine of the Den of Riechip, famed for botanical specimens, access is gained to the Grews' Well and Ben-e-challie.

Butterstone House is a fine building on the right, and is noted as being the last place of residence in Scotland of the Right Hon. W. E. Gladstone. The venerable statesman spent a month there in 1898 as the guest of Lord Armitstead. and expressed repeatedly his admiration of the beauty of the district, a favourite drive being that into Dunkeld, four miles distant.

The next place of interest is Cardney House, finely situated, with the rocky heights of Craig Mohr showing behind. This house occupies the site of an ancient hunting seat of the Kings of Scotland, the "Old Ha'" or the "Kings' Kitchen." The Loch of Craiglush is to the left, a charming sheet of water connected with the Loch o' the Lowes by a canal. Soon after the Fungarth Braes appear, with the golf club-house perched in a delightful situation. A walk back to Dunkeld may either follow the course of the highway or, passing through Fungarth, descend abruptly into Dunkeld, both routes offering many picturesque and lovely glimpses of the surrounding scenery.

These walks, and others described in previous chapters, do not by any means exhaust the walks to be found in the district. They but give an indication of the variety offered. There are innumerable charming nooks, sheltered hollows, winding paths near and far which the ardent seeker may easily find and explore. The charm of Dunkeld largely lies in its diversity. Its scenic beauty has been recognised for ages and disputed by none. All who pass may see. Other places may have higher mountains, larger waterfalls or lochs and wider woods, but seldom in such a small compass is there to be found craggy hills and wooded heights, open moorlands and flower-bedecked woods, flowing rivers, placid lakes and roaring waterfalls. Then in Dunkeld itself there are re-

minders of ancient glories when " Sainted Columb first the
Cross displayed and all Pictavia bowed," or " mitred priests
adored in lordly state." Nor is there wanting evidence of
past strife when " its ivy-clad Cathedral was reft of glory "
or " Highland claymore and Lowland spear reddened in
intestine fray."

These days are past, but memories remain and help to
strengthen the hold which Dunkeld has on its sons and
daughters who regard with pride its past history. Even when
far away, they see in dreams that little Highland city, en-
throned amongst hills on the banks of the Tay, and long to be
there. In the language of the song, " In Exile " (words and
music by G. K. Scott, Inver), they sigh:

> " In my dreams I often wander
> By Braan's roaring, rocky stream,
> Oft I gaze on Tay's calm grandeur,
> But, alas! 'tis but a dream!"

Others feel the charm and attraction, too, both of its scenery
and history, and so Dunkeld, once the capital of an ancient
kingdom, can never lose its interest, nor cease to fascinate all
lovers of Scotland's hills and history.